The Master Builder's Blueprint for Building Enduring Wealth

Dr. Gwen E. Brannum

The Master Builder's Blueprint for Building Enduring Wealth

Published by Gwen Brannum Ministries, LLC

Raleigh, North Carolina 27616

Copyright © 2024 by Gwen E. Brannum

International Standard Book Numbers

ISBN 978-1-964349-02-2 (eBook)

ISBN 978-1-964349-00-8 (Hardback)

ISBN 978-1-964349-01-5 (Paperback)

Originally Published: April 10, 2024

Published expanded version: September 10, 2024.

Dedication

This book is dedicated to three spiritually wealthy Christians who I met traveling the path of enduring wealth in 1983: Mother M. Temple (Church Leader, Chief Administrator, and Mentor), Sister N. Summers (Prayer Warrior, Spiritual Mother, and Mentor), and Elder P. Summers (Clergyman, Supervisor, and Mentor). During a crucial time in my life, the Lord blessed me to have three spiritual giants who nurtured me with godly wisdom, knowledge, and understanding in a manner that helped to empower me to fulfill my divine purpose. Although my unforgettable mentors have transitioned from the earthly realm to the heavenly realm, I am still reaping the dividends of their spiritual investments.

Acknowledgment

First, I acknowledge the boundless Master Builder who owns the blueprint for my life. As His design for my life continues to unfold, the Lord Jesus Christ blessed me to meet three extraordinary women who faithfully collaborated with me in the rain, sleet, and snow canvassing neighborhoods, parks, and the marketplace - winning souls for Christ. In addition to being soul winners, ministers, prayer warriors, marketplace workers, and members of Apostolic Pentecostal Truth Ministry, Inc. (located in Maryland); Minister P. Summers, Evangelist S. Schools, and Minister B. Walker worked faithfully at GB Unique Designs (religious gifts and hats store). Also, the three God-fearing women worked diligently at various fundraiser sites to help generate funds to purchase the first property owned by the church in Waldorf, Maryland. To God be the glory for allowing me to have the privilege to work with three amazing godly women who helped to propel me into greater heights at the start of my pastoring journey.

Traveling with the boundless Master Builder to greater dimensions of wealth, I successfully completed and submitted my dissertation entitled: "The Master Builder's Blueprint for Building Enduring Wealth" in fulfillment of the Doctor of Philosophy in Christian Business – November 23, 2023. To God be the glory!

Preface

In a world driven by the relentless pursuit of wealth and prosperity, there exists a timeless blueprint, a divine plan conceived by the infinite Master Builder—the Creator of all things, both seen and unseen. This book, "The Master Builder's Blueprint for Building Enduring Wealth," unveils the profound principles embedded in the very fabric of existence, guiding seekers towards a wealth that transcends temporal assets.

The Master Builder's invitation, as seen in Matthew 11:28-29, reverberates through the ages, beckoning the weary and burdened to find rest in Him. Originally extended to a people ensnared by legalistic constraints, this invitation remains ever relevant during this Grace Age Dispensation, resonating with diligent seekers worldwide.

Faith-filled obedience is a prerequisite for finding rest—a rest that empowers believers to embark on the path of enduring wealth. By God's design, this wealth leads to the ultimate prosperous destination in eternity. To tread this path successfully, one must set his or her affection on eternal wealth, cultivating a spiritual mind capable of comprehending divine secrets that elude the unspiritual.

The wisdom of God, bestowed upon the spiritually minded, becomes indispensable for navigating the nuances of wealth. The thoughts of Christ, embedded in the believer's mind, are a compass on the journey of enduring prosperity. Without them, the risk of succumbing to erroneous ideas about wealth arises, perpetuating myths such as God's aversion to His people prospering or the inherent evil in desiring financial abundance.

As believers navigate the path of enduring wealth, they must guard against the allure of temporal riches, avoiding a shift from spiritual to carnal mindedness. Fearing God and keeping His commandments emerge as crucial safeguards against spiritual death, ensuring alignment with the Spirit's desires rather than succumbing to the flesh's impulses.

The Master Builder's blueprint offers direction not only for spiritual prosperity but also for the holistic well-being of believers— spiritually, socially, physically, emotionally, and mentally. It is a guide to thriving in the marketplace, where the Master Builder seeks individuals from all levels of society, inviting them to experience enduring wealth.

This book delves into the profound truths of the Master Builder's blueprint, offering insights into the divine principles that, when followed faithfully, lead to a wealth that surpasses all understanding. May these pages serve as a lantern on your journey, illuminating the path towards the enduring wealth that the Master Builder graciously bestows upon those who heed His call.

Contents

Chapter 1

Introduction

The infinite Master Builder is the source of all wealth. Therefore, He owns the blueprint for prospering both spiritually and naturally. Contrary to God's wealth-building principles, humans seek to build wealth using their finite power. Without experiencing the power of the Holy Spirit, humans work continuously to prosper in every dimension of wealth, but they are restless, heavily laden, and spiritually poor. Nevertheless, as seen in Matthew 11:28-30, the Master Builder extends an open invitation saying:

> Come to me, all you who are weary and burdened, and I will give you rest. Take my yoke upon you and learn from me, for I am gentle and humble in heart, and you will find rest for your souls. For my yoke is easy and my burden is light.[1]

Although the Master Builder's invitation was to the Jews during the Law Dispensation, it is still valid during this Grace Age Dispensation. Originally, the invitation seen in the eleventh chapter of Matthew was for a group of people who were struggling to adhere to an abundance of rules and regulations. Trying to fulfill the

---

[1] Matthew 11:28 & 30 - New International Version (NIV).

burdensome regulations that came from the Rabbinical Law, the people were exhausted and heavily laden. Offering to alleviate the Jews' burden, Jesus invites them to come and find rest in Him.[2]

Not only did the Jews need to find rest in Jesus, but every human who enters this world needs the rest that Jesus offers. Knowing the needs of all humans, the Master Builder constructed an invitation that extends far past the Law Dispensation. Miraculously, the resounding echoes of the invitation are loud and clear in this Grace Age Dispensation. Moving closer to the sound of the Master Builder's invite, diligent seekers all over the world are responding in faith-filled obedience.

Since faith-filled obedience pleases God, He faithfully fulfills His promise by allowing true believers to find rest in Him. Having the long overdue rest needed since birth, believers are strengthened, energized, and fortified to follow the Master Builder on the path of enduring wealth. By God's design, the path of enduring wealth leads to the ultimate wealthy place located in eternity. To reach the ultimate wealthy place, faith-filled followers must "set [their] affection on things above, not on things on the earth."[3]

---

[2] Matthew 11:28 - New International Version (NIV).

[3] Colossians 3:2 - King James Version (KJV).

Staying focused on the things above gives vent to remaining spiritually minded. The spiritual mind readily receives divine secrets that are inconceivable to unspiritual minds. While the unspiritual mind leans to its own understanding, the spiritual mind is open to receiving godly wisdom. The wisdom of God cultivates the spiritual mind to receive and act upon the wealth building principles of God. In addition, the wisdom of God reveals the necessity of maintaining a spiritual mind. Mainly because as seen in 1 Corinthians 2:14-16:

> . . . *the unspiritual* [person] *simply cannot accept the matters which the Spirit deals with—they just* [do not] *make sense to* [him or her], . . . [an individual] *must be spiritual to see spiritual things. The spiritual* [person], *on the other hand, has an insight into the meaning of everything, though* [his or her] *insight may baffle the* [worldly person]. *This is because the former is sharing in God's wisdom. Who has known the mind of the Lord that* [he or she] *may instruct Him? Incredible as it may sound, we who are spiritual have the very thoughts of Christ!* [4]

The thoughts of Christ are essential for staying on the path of enduring wealth.

Without the thoughts of Christ saturating our minds, it is easy to be deceived by erroneous ideas about wealth. There are two

---

[4] 1 Corinthians 2:14-16 - J. B. Phillips New Testament (PHILLIPS).

common erroneous ideas about prosperity: 1) God does not want His people to prosper, and 2) the desire to have vast amounts of money is evil. Of course, neither of the ideas is true because God desires to prosper His people in every dimension of wealth. In fact, to effectively fulfill the will of God, believers must prosper both spiritually and naturally.

Having experienced both spiritual and natural prosperity, Apostle Paul encourages believers in Philippians 4:19 by saying:

> *Know this: my God will also fill every need you have according to His glorious riches in Jesus the Anointed, our Liberating King.*[5]

Today, all Christians can rejoice because "this same God. . .will supply all [our] needs from His glorious riches, which have been given to us in Christ Jesus"[6]

Prospering both spiritually and naturally happens when Christians continue to follow Christ Jesus in the path of enduring wealth. However, believers must guard against overly focusing on temporal wealth. Being obsessed with prospering naturally is a sure sign the believer has shifted from having a spiritual mindset to having a carnal mindset. To have a carnal mindset means an individual is failing to trust God wholeheartedly. So, to regain a

---

[5] Philippians 4:19 - The Voice (VOICE).

[6] Philippians 4:19 - New Living Translation (NLT).

spiritual mindset, an individual must submit to the plan and purposes of God.

Once an individual regains a spiritual mindset, he or she must diligently guard against the pitfall of leaning to his or her own understanding. At all times, believers must commit to viewing things from God's perspective. Furthermore, believers must consistently follow God's protocol for preserving a spiritual mindset. Two key ingredients for maintaining a spiritual mindset are: 1) having a genuine respect for the sovereignty of God and 2) keeping God's commandments.

The command to fear God and keep His commandments is one of the overarching themes of the Bible. Of course, trillions of messages have yet to be preached about respecting the sovereignty of God and adhering to His commands. But:

> *When all has been heard, the end of the matter is: fear God - worship Him with awe-filled reverence, knowing that He is almighty God and keep His commandments, for this applies to every person. For God will bring every act to judgment, every hidden and secret thing, whether it is good or evil.*

As seen in Ecclesiastes 12:13-14, no one is excluded from having a genuine respect for the sovereignty of God and keeping His commandments.

Failing to fear God and refusing to keep His commandments is, in fact, spiritual death. To be clear, the Master Builder's blueprint reveals:

Those who live according to the flesh have their minds set on what the flesh desires; but those who live in accordance with the Spirit have their minds set on what the Spirit desires. The mind governed by the flesh is death, but the mind governed by the Spirit is life and peace. The mind governed by the flesh is hostile to God; it does not submit to God's law, nor can it do so. Those who are in the realm of the flesh cannot please God.[7]

Romans 8:5-8 clearly reveals how operating in the realm of the flesh happens when an individual leans to his or her own finite understanding.

Engrossed in their own thoughts, carnal minded individuals strategize ways to fulfill "the lust of the flesh, and the lust of the eyes, and the pride of life."[8] As a result, the carnal minded individual strays further away from the things of God. Straying off the path of enduring wealth, the carnal minded individual aimlessly wonders down paths that lead only to temporal wealth. Not willing to leave the carnal minded individual on an unauthorized path, the gentle and humble hearted Master Builder re-invites the carnal minded individual to follow Him.

---

[7] Romans 8:5-8 - New International Version (NIV).

[8] 1 John 2:16 - King James Version (KJV).

Following the Master Builder takes the guesswork out of life. He is thoroughly aware of all the paths in life. In fact, He takes pleasure in directing the paths of faith-filled followers. Along the way, He consistently strengthens, energizes, and fortifies His people to increase spiritually and mentally. Having the necessary spiritual and mental wealth, faith-filled followers of Christ Jesus can resist the distractions that are in the world.

Refusing to be diverted, faith-filled followers keep gazing at the Author and Finisher of their faith. Steadfastly, looking unto Jesus, Christians remain consciously aware of the insight revealed in 1 John 2:16-17:

> *...all that is in the world—the lust and sensual craving of the flesh and the lust and longing of the eyes and the boastful pride of life [pretentious confidence in one's resources or in the stability of earthly things]—these do not come from the "Father" but are from the world. The world is passing away, and with it its lusts [the shameful pursuits and ungodly longings]; but the one who does the will of God and [fulfills] His purposes - lives forever.*[9]

Consistently doing the will of God and fulfilling His purposes, faith-

---

[9] 1 John 2:16-17- Amplified Bible (AMP).

filled followers are determined to follow the boundless Master Builder on the path of enduring wealth.

While faithfully following the Master Builder, believers continue to prosper both spiritually and naturally. Natural prosperity includes distinct aspects of life such as educational, emotional, financial, mental, physical, and social. Although God allows His followers to prosper in the natural realm, the greatest prosperity is spiritual wealth. At all times, the Master Builder releases both spiritual and natural prosperity to reveal His glory and give insight.

As God reveals His glory in the lives of His people, unbelievers become inquisitive. Of course, when unbelievers start inquiring, believers have an opportunity to direct others to the Master Builder. Directing souls to Christ proves to be a blessing for both the believer as well as the unbeliever. When believers point souls to Christ, they are encouraging unbelievers to seek help from the Self-existing God. The very moment an unbeliever makes a conscious effort to seek help from God, the trajectory of his or her life changes. The greater blessing comes when unbelievers go through the process of changing from an unbeliever to becoming a true believer.

Although unbelievers cannot build spiritual wealth, God allows them to prosper from a natural perspective. However, the moment an unbeliever becomes a true believer and yokes up with the Master Builder, he or she has the capacity to prosper both spiritually and naturally. With that thought in mind, it is important to mention – God desires to prosper people on all levels in society. In fact, the Master Builder is in the business of instructing and counseling people from all social classes to prosper in every dimension of wealth.

Prospering both spiritually and naturally serves as a reminder that the Master Builder "satisfies the thirsty and fills the hungry with good things."[10] He desires to satisfy individuals in every sphere of the marketplace. At this very moment, the gentle and humble hearted Master Builder is looking for board members, shareholders, corporate officers, executive officers, and frontline employees to satisfy with good things. While the Master Builder is seeking faithful followers who have an integral role in the marketplace, He has no respect of persons.[11] Therefore, His invitation extends far past the business world and the corporate world.

Throughout the entire world, regardless of one's economic status or background, he or she can accept the Master Builder's

---

[10] Psalm 107:9 - New International Version (NIV).

[11] Romans 2:11 - King James Version (KJV).

invitation. Once an individual accepts the Master Builder's invitation, he or she immediately enters the path of enduring wealth. However, accepting the invitation is not just a superficial belief that there is one God. Remember, James 2:19 states, "you believe that there is one God. Good!"[12]

Believing there is one God is terrific. But there is more to accepting the Master Builder's invitation than believing there is one God.

> *Are there still some among you who hold that "only believing" is enough? . . . Well, remember that the demons believe this too—so strongly that they tremble in terror!*[13]

Although demons believe and shudder, they do not have the capacity to be true believers who are spiritually minded. Therefore, demons cannot follow the plan of God. Nevertheless, belief is part of God's divine order for entering the path of enduring wealth.

Another part of God's divine order is for humans to use their freedom of choice. For example, humans must freely choose to follow the Master Builder in the path of enduring wealth. To solidify the choice, believers must fulfill the God-ordained prerequisites.

---

[12] James 2:19 - New International Version (NIV).

[13] James 2:19 - Living Bible (TLB).

First, anyone who comes to God must believe that He exist. Coupled with belief in the existence of God, diligent seekers who are looking to receive God's conditional promises must exercise faith.

By God's design, receiving the promise of salvation requires faith. Ephesians 2:8 declares:

> For it is by grace [God's remarkable compassion and favor drawing you to Christ] that you have been saved [delivered from judgment and given eternal life] through faith. And this [salvation] is not of yourselves [not through your own effort], but it is the [undeserved, gracious] gift of God.

Despite the condition of today's world, the gift of God is still available! By the grace of God, finite humans who are enslaved to sin, can receive God's gift of redemption through faith.

To be clear, the only way finite humans can receive the gift of God - is to please Him with faith. Leaving no room for error, in Hebrews 11:6, the Master Builder left on record:

> *You can never please God without faith, without depending on Him. Anyone who wants to come to God must believe that there is a God and that He rewards those who look for Him.*[14]

---

[14] Hebrews 11:6 - Living Bible (TLB).

So, without exceptions, every diligent seeker who comes to God desiring to be redeemed from the grip of spiritual poverty must demonstrate faith.

Likewise, anyone desiring to prosper both spiritually and naturally must use faith to receive all three parts of the Master Builder's invitation: 1) to find rest in Him, 2) to follow Him, and 3) to build with Him. Furthermore, to reap the ongoing benefits of the three-part invitation, Christians must consistently please God with faith.

> *What is faith? It is the confident assurance that something we want is going to happen. It is the certainty that what we hope for is waiting for us, even though we cannot see it up ahead.*[15]

So, to please God, we must demonstrate absolute conviction that there are realities in the plan and purposes of God that we have never seen.

The moment a diligent seeker pleases God with faith, he or she can enjoy the realities of God's plan and purposes by entering a partnership with the Master Builder. The partnership gives true believers direct access to God's wealth building blueprint. As a

---

[15] Hebrews 11:1 - Living Bible (TLB).

result, Christians are authorized to begin building enduring wealth immediately. But just as there are natural building laws, there are also spiritual building laws. For example, in the natural realm, humans establish and ratify laws, codes, and procedures to assure buildings are conducive for occupancy.

In the spiritual realm, God has established laws that determine if He will make His aboard within an individual. Unlike natural laws, God's laws are "ever settled in heaven."[16] So, based on God's established laws, He determines if the life of an individual is conducive for His Holy Spirit to occupy. When the Spirit of God occupies the life of the believer, He authorizes the believer to build according to His plan.

Prior to receiving God's approval, a person must go through a rebuilding phase. The good news is - the Master Builder oversees the reconstruction process. First, a true and tried foundation is laid in the heart of the believer. Remember, the only true and tried foundation for the innermost being of humans is Jesus Christ. Amazingly, the Master Builder - places Himself in the innermost being of an individual.

Having a sure foundation established, the Master Builder

---

[16] Psalm 119:89 - King James Version (KJV).

reconstructs, quickens, and makes alive the individual's spirit. Something wonderful happens when we are made alive in Christ Jesus! 1 Peter 2:5 & 9 declares:

> [we are] *as lively stones,* [we are] *built up a spiritual house, a holy priesthood, to offer up spiritual sacrifices, acceptable to God by Jesus Christ. . .* [we are also] *a chosen generation, a royal priesthood, a holy nation, a peculiar people; that* [we] *should* [show] *forth the praises of Him who hath called* [us] *out of darkness into His marvelous light.*[17]

Remaining in God's marvelous light, believers gain greater insight concerning the Master Builder's wealth-building principles. In addition, as believers walk in the light of God's countenance, they realized the importance of abiding in Christ.

The only way Christians can bear fruit in every dimension of wealth, we must abide in the true Vine. The Master Builder, who is the true Vine, said:

> *Remain in Me, and I will remain in you. Just as no branch can bear fruit by itself without remaining in the vine, neither can you bear fruit, producing evidence of your faith unless*

---

[17] 1 Peter 2:5 & 9 - King James Version (KJV).

you remain in Me.[18]

Remaining in the Master Builder gives vent to the believer trusting in the Lord with all his or her heart.

As the believer exudes confident trust in the Master Builder, He abides within the innermost being of the believer. While making His aboard, the Master Builder cultivates the believer's thoughts, speech, and actions. During the cultivation process, the believer receives a wealth of wisdom, knowledge, and understanding. As a result, the believer is divinely fortified to follow the plan and purposes of God. Philippians 2:13 declares:

> *God is at work within [the believer], helping [the believer]*
> *to obey [God], and then helping [the believer] do what*
> *[God] wants.*[19]

Doing what God wants includes reverencing Him and keeping His commandments.

However, to have profound respect for God and to genuinely love Him, an individual must become a new creation in Christ Jesus. 2 Corinthians 5:17 emphatically states:

---

[18] John 15:4 - Amplified Bible (AMP).

[19] Philippians 2:13 - Living Bible (TLB).

If anyone is in Christ [that is, grafted in, joined to Him by faith in Him as Savior], [he or she] is a new creature [reborn and renewed by the Holy Spirit]; the old things [the previous moral and spiritual condition] have passed away. Behold, new things have come [because spiritual awakening brings a new life].[20]

Having a new life requires a new heart.

When the Master Builder remakes an individual, He removes the old stony heart and constructs a new heart within the believer. The new heart matches the Master Builder's blueprint. By God's design, the new heart is full of God's love. As a result, believers have the capacity to love the One:

who gave Himself for us, that He might redeem us from every lawless deed and purify for Himself His own special people, zealous for good works.[21]

Having redemption from ungodliness and worldly passions, Spirit-filled believers can consistently live godly, soberly, and righteously.

Righteous living is an ongoing requirement for pleasing God. Although the Master Builder commands His followers to be

----

[20] 2 Corinthians 5:17 - Amplified Bible (AMP).

[21] Titus 2:14 - New King James Version (NKJV).

righteous, He does not accept self-righteousness. Mainly because self-righteousness diabolically opposes the Master Builder's blueprint for building spiritual wealth. Therefore, it is important to have a clear understanding about being in right standing with God.

Being in right standing with God does not happen through self-righteousness. Contrary to God's blueprint, self-righteousness is a grandiose view of one's own ideologies and it is the breeding ground for making provision for the flesh regarding its improper desires. In an article entitled, *Righteousness vs. Unrighteousness*, Leon F. Seltzer, PhD states:

> *Self-righteousness is giving final authority for one's decisions not to God but to* [the person's own selfish desires]. *So, self-righteousness becomes, paradoxically, a kind of self-trusting sacrilege: the person* [is not] *serving God's will but profaning God by serving, or taking final direction from, themselves.* [22]

On the other hand, being in right standing with God means an individual has put on the Lord Jesus Christ. Therefore, he or she has

---

[22] https://www.psychologytoday.com/us/blog/evolution-the-self/202101/righteous-vs-self-righteous

been clothed with the righteousness of God.[23] To maintain a right standing with God, an individual must walk by faith, reverence God, and keep His commandments.

Without having on the righteousness of God, self-righteous individuals follow the path that seems right for fulfilling "the lust of the flesh, the lust of the eyes, and the pride of life."[24] Filled with arrogance, self-righteous individuals joyfully walk in the flesh ignoring the divine order of God. In fact, they build wealth by leaning on their own understanding. "Sure, [self-righteous] people appear to be having a good time, but all that laughter will end in heartbreak."[25] Mainly because the Master Builder does not validate or reward any form of self-righteousness.

The only righteousness that has God's approval is His righteousness alone. John Piper informs, "God's righteousness consists in His unswerving commitment always to act for the glory of His name. . ."[26] With that thought in mind, God is at work in every sphere of the marketplace to bring glory and honor to His name.

---

[23] Romans 13:14 - King James Version (KJV).

[24] 1 John 2:16 - King James Version (KJV).

[25] Proverbs 14:13 - The Message (MSG).

[26] Piper, John. The Justification of God.

Piper further explains:

> *God's commitment to maintaining the glory and honor of His name is ultimate. His saving acts are righteous acts, not merely because they uphold the covenant promises, but because they preserve and display the honor of God's name.*[27]

Even in the marketplace, God is working things after the counsel of His own will to preserve and display the honor of His name.

On an individual level, God is working in the lives of Christian workers so they can - glorify Him and bring honor to His name. Not just in the marketplace, but in every dimension of wealth. However, Piper explains:

> *What determines whether* [an individual] *glorifies God one way or the other is not* [predicated on his or her self-righteousness] . . ., *but* [his or her] *faith in the promises of God. Since faith pleases God, He faithfully, . . . manifests His righteousness in keeping His promises to those who believe, for in this He displays the value of His glory by blessing those whose stance of faith renders His glory and*

---

[27] Piper, John. The Justification of God (p. 112).

righteousness most conspicuous.[28]

As seen throughout the Bible, individuals who please the Lord experience the fulfillment of God's promises.

When God manifest His righteousness through fulfilled promises, believers prosper both spiritually and naturally. But it is important to note, God's righteousness is also revealed in His vengeance. Piper puts it like this:

> [God] *also manifests His righteousness in punishing those who remain in unbelief.* [Because all] *unbelief is the gravest assault on God and to bless it indefinitely would be to deny the infinite value of His glorious trustworthiness.*[29]

Remember, God's blueprint for building enduring wealth requires Christians to trust in the Lord wholeheartedly.

Unlike saintly trust, unbelief is deeply rooted in the individual's unholy nature. Therefore, the Master Builder removes the root cause of unbelief by laying a righteous and enduring foundation. Watch the process. First, the Master Builder removes the dilapidated foundation and lays a new foundation by imparting and imputing the righteousness of God. Miraculously, somewhere

---

[28] Piper, John. The Justification of God (pp. 133-134).

[29] Piper, John. The Justification of God (p. 134).

during the imparting and imputing process, the believer yokes up with the Master Builder.

When the believer yokes up with the Lord Jesus, he or she becomes empowered to obey the commandments of God. While obeying all of God's commandments are essential, there are two laws that are the greatest commandments of all. As seen in Matthew 22:37-40, Jesus said:

> *Love the Lord your God with all your heart and with all your soul and with all your mind. This is the first and greatest commandment. And the second is like it: Love your neighbor as yourself. All the Law and the Prophets hang on these two commandments.*[30]

The two undergirding laws that endorsed the Old Testament are just as important in the New Testament. So much so, every covenant relevant to God's Church are commandments built on the principles of loving God and loving others. No one can love God without loving others. In fact, 1 John 4:20 states:

> *if a man says, I love God, and hates his brother, he is a liar: for he, that loveth not his brother whom he hath seen, how*

---

[30] Matthew 22:37-40 - New International Version (NIV).

can he love God whom he hath not seen?[31]

In John 15:12, Jesus said, "this is my commandment, that you love one another as I have loved you."[32] Prior to giving the command for us to love one another, in John 14:23, Jesus informs His followers, ". . . if a man loves me, he will keep my words. . ."[33]

To keep the Master Builder's words, humans need to be infused with God's love. Now, the subject matter of being filled with God's love highlights the need for having a new heart. More especially since it is impossible to love God with the sinful heart. The only solution is to receive a new heart designed by the Master Builder. According to Romans 5:5, the Holy Spirit pours God's love into the believer's heart.

Once the believer's heart is filled with the love of God, he or she immediately receives the catalyst for loving God and loving others. The love of God also enables believers to keep God's commandments. As believers adhere to God's wealth building principles, they are illuminated and fortified to walk after the Spirit. Of course, following the Holy Spirit is a sure way to gain spiritual

---

[31] 1 John 4:20 - King James Version (KJV).

[32] John 15:12 - English Standard Version (ESV).

[33] John 14:23 - King James Version (KJV).

wealth.

Walking after the Spirit is also key to staying on the path of enduring wealth. While following the Holy Spirit, believers consistently gain strength to fulfill the righteousness of the law.[34] However, during the Law Dispensation humans could not find the strength to live according to the Law. Why? Because they had contaminated hearts, and they needed the indwelling power of the Holy Spirit.

Careful observation of the Bible reveals the contamination of humans' hearts happened long before the Law Dispensation. Sadly, the Dispensation of Conscious opened with humans having deceitful and desperately wicked hearts.[35] After the "Fall of Adam," all humans entered the world needing a new heart and a new mind. But through the mouth of Ezekiel, God proclaims the good news concerning humans having the opportunity to receive new hearts and new minds.

Without assistance from cardiologists, neurologists, or psychologists, people throughout the world are miraculously receiving new hearts and new minds. Like Nicodemus, there are

---

[34] Romans 8:4 - King James Version (KJV).

[35] Jeremiah 17:9 - King James Version (KJV).

people who stand amazed asking, "how can these things be?"[36] Well, in Ezekiel 36:26-27 the omniscient Creator answers by saying:

I will give you a new heart and a new mind. I will take away your stubborn heart of stone and give you an obedient heart. I will put My Spirit in you and will see to it that you follow My laws and keep all the commands I have given you.[37]

Although the dispensation of the grace of God was not revealed in the Old Testament, God is true to His Word.[38]

In today's Grace Age Dispensation, humans can follow the Plan of Salvation and receive new hearts and new minds. As a result, believers can do whatever God commands. When a Christian faithfully adheres to God's principles, he or she develops a greater adoration for God. Out of love and adoration for God, Christians "set [their] affection on things above, not on things on the earth."[39]

The Christian who sets his or her affection on building wealth according to the Master Builder's blueprint reaps countless spiritual and natural benefits. The benefits of obeying God's laws

---

[36] John 3:9 - New International Version (NIV).

[37] Ezekiel 36:26-27 - Good News Translation (GNT).

[38] Ephesians 3:2-6 - King James Version (KJV).

[39] Colossians 3:2 - King James Version (KJV).

and doing whatever He commands supersede our greatest prayers. Ephesians 3:20-21 put it like this:

> *God can do anything, you know - far more than you could ever imagine or guess or request in your wildest dreams! He does it not by pushing us around but by working within us.*[40]

With that thought in mind, God is at work in the marketplace, working within board members, shareholders, corporate officers, executive officers, and frontline employees for His glory.

As the Master Builder works within marketplace Christians, He imparts revelational knowledge and gives illumination concerning His wealth building principles. According to God's blueprint, it is important to know the differences between enduring wealth, natural wealth, and riches. In reference to natural wealth, it is worth noting that riches are different from the general concept of wealth. For example, riches can be a grandiose display of enormous amounts of money, expensive clothes, mansions, and moneymaking businesses. On the other hand, Lindsley and Bradley informs:

> *Wealth includes adequate physical possessions to live and flourish as a human being created in the image of God, and it also requires a specific heart and attitude toward the*

---

[40] Ephesians 3:20-21 - The Message (MSG).

Gwen E. Brannum

purpose of possessions.[41]

To have the right attitude toward the purpose of earthly wealth, an individual must be in partnership with the Master Builder. The invitation to enter a partnership with the Master Builder is still in effect. Jesus Christ is still inviting individuals from all social classes to:

> *Come to Me, all who are weary and heavily burdened [by religious rituals that provide no peace], and I will give you rest [refreshing your souls with salvation]. Take My yoke upon you and learn from Me [following Me as My disciple], for I am gentle and humble in heart, and you will find rest (renewal, blessed quiet) for your souls. For My yoke is easy [to bear] and My burden is light.*[42]

Are you burdened by religious rituals or the cares of this world?

Whatever the burden may be, Jesus said, ". . . I will give you rest."[43] According to the Ellicott's Commentary:

> *The 'I' is emphasized in the Greek. He alone gives what no*

---

[41] For the Least of These by Art Lindsley and Anne Bradley (pp. 60-61).

[42] Matthew 11:28-30 - Amplified Bible (AMP).

[43] Matthew 11:28 - New International Version (NIV).

one else can give. [Jesus Christ removes] *the burden of sin* [and frees restless humans] *from the weariness of fruitless toil.*[44]

As seen throughout the Bible, outside of Christ Jesus, humans are toiling unsuccessfully to alleviate the strain of being spiritually debilitated and fruitless.

The weariness of fruitless toil has plagued humans since the fall of the first Adam. Nevertheless, the second Adam who is the Master Builder - invites all who are weary and heavily burdened to come to Him, and He will give rest. Not only will He alleviate the burden and give rest, but He will also teach His faithful followers how to stay free from the yoke of bondage. Notice the first words of Jesus in Matthew 11:29, "take my yoke upon you." On the surface, the thought of yoking up might sound like bondage. But on the contrary, the Master Builder is inviting humans to experience true freedom.

There is no true freedom without yoking up with the Master Builder and learning from Him. Every aspect of Jesus' teachings offers freedom. For example, Jesus offers freedom from agonizing religious burdens. Such as seen in Matthew 11:29. Various

---

[44] https://biblehub.com/matthew/11-28.htm.

commentators highlight, "the teaching of the Pharisees was a yoke too grievous to be borne."[45] But the Pharisees were not the only ones who burdened the people with their unbearable teachings. Matthew 23:4 clearly states:

> *The Scribes and Pharisees tie up heavy loads [that are hard to bear] and place them on men's shoulders, but they themselves will not lift a finger [to make them lighter].*[46]

But Jesus, having compassion on the people, extends an invitation to yoke up with Him.

What is the yoke of Jesus Christ? One commentator informs, "the yoke of Christ is His teaching, His rule of life, [as] explained by the "learn of Me" that follows."[47] Interestingly, the only way an individual can truly learn from Jesus Christ is to yoke up with Him. Yoking up with Him means the believer has accepted the Master Builder's three-part invitation: to rest in Him, to follow Him, and to build with Him. Once believers yoke up with the Master Builder, He gives them knowledge and understanding concerning His wealth-building principles. In addition, the Master Builder gives the true

---

[45] https://biblehub.com/commentaries/ellicott/matthew/11.htm.

[46] Matthew 23:4 - Amplified Bible (AMP).

[47] https://biblehub.com/commentaries/ellicott/matthew/11.htm.

believer godly wisdom so he or she can properly apply His principles.

When Christians properly apply the Master Builders wealth building principles, they prosper both spiritually and naturally. From a spiritual perspective, God enables Christians to maintain an upright stance in every dimension of wealth. Just as God provides structure, regulation, and balance in Nature, He provides divine balance and structure for Christians. As a result, believers grow in grace and are strengthened to faithfully follow five major wealth-building principles: 1) seeking God first in every season of life, 2) trusting the Lord wholeheartedly, 3) always acknowledging the Lord, 4) glorifying God in every dimension of wealth, and 5) remembering the infinite Master Builder is the source of all wealth.

Since God is the source of all wealth, He is the only One who is qualified to prosper His people in every dimension of wealth. In fact, He is the only One who can simultaneously supply the needs of billions and trillions of people despite the seasons of life. Unceasingly, the boundless Master Builder knows how to open the spiritual eyes of diligent seekers, give revelational knowledge, and ongoing illumination as He prospers His people both spiritually and naturally.

Chapter 2

The Infinite Master Builder

The infinite Master Builder who owns everything is willing and able to convey wealthy portions of what He owns without ever becoming depleted. However, anyone who comes to Him seeking to receive a portion of spiritual and natural prosperity must first believe He exists. In addition, diligent seekers must believe, "[God] rewards those who earnestly seek Him."[48] As a result, He faithfully reveals His glory, gives insight, and prospers all diligent seekers who trust Him and consistently acknowledge He is infinite.

Being infinite means - the Master Builder's attributes and character are without limits. Psalm 147:5 and Psalm 90:2 declares:

Great is our Lord, and of great power: His understanding is infinite.[49]

Before the mountains were created, before the earth was formed, [He is] *God without beginning or end.*[50]

---

[48] Hebrews 11:6 - New International Version (NIV).

[49] Psalm 147:5 - Darby Translation (DARBY).

[50] Psalm 90:2 - Living Bible (TLB).

Therefore, He is the One and Only self-existing God who is immutable – He will never change. He is the Eternal One!

Since God is eternal and cannot change, that means His attributes are eternally the same. In other words, God is infinite in wisdom, knowledge, and understanding. He is eternally self-sufficient, omnipotent, omniscient, omnipresent, and omnibenevolent. Also, God is eternally faithful, glorious, good, gracious, holy, just, and merciful. He is perfect in all His ways and dependable. There are not enough words to fully describe the infinitude of God. Nevertheless, without doubt, Christians are thoroughly convinced – our God is boundless!

The infinite Master Builder demonstrated His boundless nature when He "formed, put in order, and equipped [the heavens and the earth] for their intended purpose."[51] When God "stretched the northern sky over empty space and hung the earth on nothing,"[52] He demonstrated His infinitude. Although the boundless nature of God is incomprehensible, His creative acts provide the evidence needed for humans to believe that He exists. Believing in the existence of God is a basic requirement for entering the path of

---

[51] Hebrews 11:3 - Amplified Bible (AMP).

[52] Job 26:7 - Easy-to-Read Version (ERV).

enduring wealth.

Couple with belief in the existence of God, faith is also essential for staying in the path of enduring wealth. In every season of life, faith pleases God. Despite the swift transitions of life, to please God, we must "walk by faith and not by sight."[53] Unlike belief, "Faith is the assurance of things [we] have hoped for, the absolute conviction that there are realities [we have] never seen."[54]

Reading from the Amplified Bible, Hebrews 11:1 defines faith as being:

> *the assurance (title deed, confirmation) of things hoped for (divinely guaranteed), and the evidence of things not seen - the conviction of their reality – (faith comprehends as fact what cannot be experienced by the physical senses)."* [55]

Therefore, faith is the key ingredient that causes God to manifest His promises in the lives of believers. One of the first promise all true believers received by faith is the rest that Jesus provides.

Finding rest in Jesus, intensifies our faith. So much so that

---

[53] 2 Corinthians 5:7 - New King James Version (NKJV).

[54] Hebrews 11:1 - The Voice (VOICE).

[55] Hebrews 11:1 - Amplified Bible (AMP).

when we - ask, seek, and knock, we "rest in the Lord and wait patiently for Him"[56] to fulfill His promises. In fact, Jesus promised we can:

> *Ask and it will be given to [us]; seek and [we] will find; knock and the door will be opened for [us]. For everyone who asks receives; the one who seeks finds; and to the one who knocks, the door will be opened.*[57]

So, on the authority of God's Word, we are completely convinced – "whatever [we] ask for in prayer [according to the will of God], having faith and really believing, [we] will receive."[58]

In addition to experiencing answered prayers and receiving the promises of God, by faith, Christians gain greater insight concerning the creative acts of God. For example, through the eyes of faith, we understand the entire world was made at the command of the Master Builder.[59] Romans 11:36 puts it like this:

> *For all things are from Him, by Him, and for Him. Glory*

---

[56] Psalm 37:7a - King James Version (KJV).

[57] Matthew 7:7-8 - New International Version (NIV).

[58] Matthew 21:22 - Amplified Bible, Classic Edition (AMPC).

[59] Hebrews 11:3 - New Century Version (NCV).

belongs to Him forever! Amen.

True believers are confident that God is the First and the Last - Authentic Architect, Surveyor, Builder and Maker of the universe. Without doubt, we are convinced, God eternally knows every star by name. In eternity, He declared the intended purpose of the sun, the moon, the stars, and all the other planets.

When God created the universe, He simply spoke into existence what He already had in His eternal mind. While speaking what was in His eternal mind, the Master Builder said, "let there be light, and there was light."[60] One commentator explains:

> *The Hebrew words for let there be light is yehi 'or. These are the words that were in the original writings of the Bible. Yehi 'or translates to "let there be light."*[61]

At the command of the Master Builder, light appeared. Interestingly, prior to creating the sun, the moon, and the stars, God created light. After He separated the light from the darkness, "God called the light day, and the darkness He called night. And there was evening, and

---

[60] Genesis 1:3 - New International Version (NIV).

[61] https://www.christianity.com/wiki/god/why-did-god-say-let-there-be-light.html

there was morning - the first day."[62]

As He continued to reveal His plan, "[the Master Builder] called for dry land to appear, and it was so."[63] Notice how God set the stage for the making of man from the dust of the earth. Watch the process:[64]

Day #1	God created light.	Genesis 1:1-5
Day #2	God created the sky and seas.	Genesis 1:6-8
Day #3	God created the land and plants.	Genesis 1:9-13
Day #4	God created the celestial bodies.	Genesis 1:14-19
Day #5	God created the sky creatures and sea creatures.	Genesis 1:20-23
Day #6	God created animals and humans.	Genesis 1:24-31; 2:7, 18-25
Day #7	God rested.	Genesis 2:1-3

Every facet of creation happened exactly the way the boundless Master Builder planned. Even down to when and where the trees would be placed in the Garden of Eden.

---

[62] Genesis 1:4 - New International Version (NIV).

[63] Genesis 1:9 - New International Version (NIV).

[64] International Children's Bible (ICB)

When the LORD God planted a garden in Eden - amazing things happened. Genesis 2:9 states:

> *The Lord God planted all sorts of beautiful trees there in the garden, trees producing the choicest of fruit. At the center of the garden, He placed the Tree of Life, and the Tree of Conscience, giving knowledge of Good and Bad.*[65]

Although the trees seen in Genesis 2:9 in comparison to the trees seen in Genesis 1:11-12 may raise questions, both descriptions paint an extraordinary picture of the Master Builder's creative acts.

God's creation is filled with lessons that will help propel faith-filled followers to greater heights in God. For example, on the third day, God commanded the dry land to produce vegetation, plants, and trees. Bowing to the will of God, "the land produced vegetation: plants bearing seed according to their kinds and trees bearing fruit with seed in it according to their kinds."[66] God placed the necessary seed within all fruits and vegetables so they could reproduce and perpetuate their intended purpose.

Likewise, Christians have everything necessary for them to fulfill their intended purpose. 2 Peter 1:3-4 puts it like this:

> *We have everything we need to live a life that pleases God.*

---

[65] Genesis 2:9 - Living Bible (TLB).

[66] Genesis 1:12 - New International Version (NIV).

He gave us what we need by His own power, when we learned He had invited us to share in His wonderful goodness. God made great and marvelous promises, so His nature would become part of us. Then, we could escape our evil desires and the corrupt influences of this world.[67]

Now that we partake in the very nature of God; we are free from the grip of spiritual poverty.

Christian workers are alive and prosperous because we have been "created in Christ Jesus to do good works, which God prepared in advance for us to do."[68] In other words, God has saturated marketplace Christians with His glory so we can fulfill our intended purpose. Any human or any part of creation that God saturates with His glory can fulfill His plan. For instance, when God saturated the dry earth with His brilliance, the earth fulfilled its intended purpose.

Fulfilling its intended purpose, the earth displayed the brilliance of God by yielding vegetables, plants, and fruits. However, it is important to note, the earth could only produce what God had prepared in advance. By God's design, the earth is still producing. As a result, the earth is still glorifying God. In addition, the existence of all the plants in the seas and oceans glorify the

---

[67] 2 Peter 1:3-4 - Contemporary English Version (CEV).

[68] Ephesians 2:10 - New International Version (NIV).

Builder and Maker of all things.

Through the production of vegetation, God is supplying the natural needs of humans. Every time humans reap the benefits that come from vegetables, plants, and fruit-bearing trees, God gets the glory. Even when unthankful, unholy, restless humans refuse to acknowledge the infinite Master Builder, He still gets the glory for supplying the needs of humans. Throughout the marketplace in every restaurant and in every cafeteria, God gets the glory.

In kitchens around the world, God gets the glory. On farms near and far, God gets the glory because He set the course of nature and commanded the earth to produce. He alone determined the precise vegetables, plants, and trees that would grow in every region of the earth. Therefore, in every country, in every region, and every city or town - God gets the glory. For His glory, the Master Builder equipped the sun for its intended purpose.

Fulfilling its purpose, sunlight provides the necessary energy plants need to convert carbon dioxide and water into carbohydrates and oxygen. By God's design, plant leaves take in carbon dioxide from the atmosphere and water goes into the plant roots. Being infinite in wisdom, knowledge, and understanding, God planned for the process of photosynthesis to produce carbohydrates. The entire process of creating photosynthesis, carbohydrates, vegetation, plants, and fruit trees starts with the sun fulfilling its intended purpose.

By God's design, the sun faithfully shines upon the earth, providing energy to both plants and humans. Without respect of persons, "[God] causes His sun to rise on the evil and the good and sends rain on the righteous and the unrighteous."[69] Although the intricate details of the Master Builder's providential care are beyond comprehension, believers gain insight by faith. Through the eyes of faith, Christians understand God loves all humans unconditionally and He is not willing for anyone to perish.

Furthermore, by faith, Christians also understand God is available to rescue perishing souls despite the seasons of life. In fact, we are thoroughly convinced - God is present everywhere at the same time. Without hindrance, He is available to respond to diligent seekers from all social classes. So, right now, wherever you are, the infinite Master Builder is available.

Brent Saba declares, "The infinity of God is one of the most challenging attributes to understand. The fact that [the Master Builder] is limitless and immeasurable is completely beyond comprehension."[70] Although the Master Builder's divine existence is beyond understanding, it is comforting to know – He will never change. Hebrews 13:8 declares, God is eternally - "the same

---

[69] Matthew 5:45 - New International Version (NIV).

[70] Saba, Brent. The Almighty: God's Holy Attributes & Their Meaning for Your Life (p. 24). Kindle Edition.

yesterday, today, and forever."[71]

The same infinite Master Builder mentioned in the book of Hebrews testifies about Himself in Revelation 1:8 saying:

> *I am the Alpha and the Omega the Beginning and the End, ...Who is existing forever and Who was continually existing in the past and Who is to come, the Almighty the Omnipotent, the Ruler of all.* "[72]

Looking at Hebrews 13:8 in parallel with Revelation 1:8 reveals a beautiful picture of the boundless Master Builder. Notice, the One *which is* – is the same today. The One *which was* – is the same yesterday. The One *which is to come* – is the same forever.

The One who is eternally the same is the only unchanging factor in the equation of life. He is the constant source of unshakable strength any time of day or night. Being omnipresent, He is indeed a very present help in every season of life. Therefore, Christian workers can rejoice in knowing the infinite Master Builder is available in every sphere of the marketplace. He is ever-present to reveal His glory, give insight, and prosper Christian workers.

As promised, the Master Builder faithfully works on behalf

---

[71] Hebrews 13:8 – King James Version (KJV).

[72] Revelation 1:8 - Amplified Bible (AMP).

of faith-filled followers. For His glory, He works things after the counsel of His own will. To give believers insight, He faithfully demonstrates His boundless nature in every dimension of wealth despite the seasons of life. Based on Biblical history, God has always demonstrated His boundless nature in the affairs of humans.

Not just in the affairs of humans, but in every facet of nature, the infinitude of God is being displayed. Isaiah 40:12 highlights the boundless nature of God by asking:

> *Who has measured the waters in the hollow of his hand, measured heaven with a span and calculated the dust of the earth in a measure? Weighed the mountains in scales and the hills in a balance?*[73]

The questions point to the boundless nature and attributes of God. Words like measured, calculated, and weighed, point to the infallibility of the omniscient Master Builder.

Without speculations, the Master Builder predetermined every facet of the heavens and the earth. He alone predetermined how far the sun would be from the earth. Also, He alone predetermined the space between every star. Unlike finite builders,

---

[73] Isaiah 40:12 - Amplified Bible (AMP),

the infinite Master Builder did not need a surveyor, architect, contractor, or review board. No one taught Him how to "[stretch] out the northern sky over vast reaches of emptiness; [no licensing committee gave Him permission to hang] the earth itself on nothing."[74] Since He is eternally omniscient, He knows everything there is to know.

The infinite Master Builder eternally knows just how far heaven stretches over the vast reaches of emptiness. He alone determined the width of the sea, the height of the mountains, and the depth of the foundation of the earth. Notice what He asked in Job 38:4-6:

> *Where were you when I laid the foundation of the earth? Tell Me if you know and have understanding. Who determined the measurements of the earth if you know? Or who stretched the measuring line on it? On what were its foundations fastened? Or who laid its cornerstone?*[75]

In addition to the questions seen in Job, the Bible highlights other profound questions concerning the making of the universe. Even

---

[74] Job 26:7 - The Voice (VOICE).

[75] Job 38:4-6 - English Standard Version 2016 (ESV).

today, finite humans have questions about the origination of the heavens and earth.

After careful observation of Job 38:4-6 in parallel with Isaiah 40:12, the questions seen in Isaiah 40:22 comes to my mind:

> *Who else could have done it except God, enthroned high above the earth? Who else but God could stretch out the skies as if they were a curtain, draw them tight, suspend them over our heads like the roof of a tent?*[76]

Well, the all-knowing Master Builder left a profound answer on record in Isaiah 44:24 saying: "I am the Lord, Maker of all things, who alone stretches out the heavens, who spreads out the earth by Myself."[77]

Psalm 24:1 declares, "the earth is the [Master Builder's],

and the fullness thereof; the world and they that dwell therein."[78]

God alone gets the glory for creating the heavens and the earth. All

---

[76] Isaiah 40:22 - The Voice (VOICE).

[77] Isaiah 44:24 - New International Version (NIV).

[78] Psalm 24:1 - Jubilee Bible 2000 (JUB).

the evidence concerning the making of the universe points directly to the boundless God of the universe. As a witness:

> *the heavens are telling of the glory of God; And the expanse [of heaven] is declaring the work of His hands. There is no speech, nor are there [spoken] words [from the stars]; Their voice is not heard. Yet their voice [in quiet evidence] has gone out through all the earth.* "[79]

For the duration of the universe, day after day the heavens will silently witness the creative acts of God and night after night the stars will reveal knowledge.

In His infinite wisdom, knowledge, and understanding, the Master Builder eternally knows the precise dimensions of every facet of the universe. There are people who cannot conceive the concept of God knowing the precise dimensions of the universe. However, the commentator of the Cambridge Bible for Schools and Colleges offers profound insight. For example, the commentator states:

---

[79] Psalms 19:1, 3 & 4 - Amplified Bible (AMP).

The conception of the universe as measured out by its Creator appears to include two things. There is first the idea of order, adjustment, and proportion in Nature, suggesting intelligence at work in the making of the world.[80]

The second suggestion concerning the measuring of the universe is that the Master Builder uses "His infinite power to conduct the vast operations of ordering, adjusting, and proportioning the happenings of Nature."[81] Not only did He make the universe, but He also sustains every facet of His creation. He is working things according to His plan. There are no happenings in nature that catches God by surprise. Even before the creation of the material world, the infinite Master Builder knew the precise distances between every point on, above, and below the earth's surface.

Furthermore, before He separated the waters, He predetermined all the space above the water, known as airspace. Supporting this truth, Psalms 74:17 informs; the boundless Master Builder "defined and established all the borders of the earth - the divisions of land and sea. . . ."[82] Being the only infinite Builder and

---

[80] https://biblehub.com/commentaries/isaiah/40-12.htm.

[81] https://biblehub.com/commentaries/isaiah/40-12.htm.

[82] Psalms 74:17 - Amplified Bible (AMP).

Maker of all things, "He assigned to the sea its limit, so that the waters might not transgress His command."[83] Unlike finite builders, surveyors, and architects who are prone to calculation errors, the Master Builder's measurements are infallible.

The infinite Master Builder who "measured the waters in the hollow of his hand"[84] is eternally omnipresent. Being eternally omnipresent means – God is and will always be present everywhere simultaneously. A. W. Tozer informs, "the word present, of course, means here, close to, next to, and the prefix omni gives it universality."[85] Furthermore, Tozer declares, there are only few other truths taught in the Scriptures that have great clarity like the doctrine of the divine omnipresence.[86]

Although the Bible is filled with different themes, the principle of divine omnipresence is one of the supreme themes of the Scriptures. From Genesis to Revelation, in every chapter and verse – the omnipresence of God is clearly displayed. Testifying to His own omnipresence, God left on record:

---

[83] Proverbs 8:29 - English Standard Version (ESV).

[84] Isaiah 40:12 - Amplified Bible (AMP). Amplified Bible (AMP).

[85] A.W. Tozer, The Knowledge of the Holy, Series Book 2, (p. 87).

[86] Tozer, Book 2) (p. 87).

Can a man hide himself in secret places so that I cannot see him? declares the Lord. Do I not fill heaven and earth? declares the Lord.[87]

Since God fills all space, time, and eternity, there is absolutely no place for humans or anything else to be out of His sight.

In Isaiah 43:2, God makes it clear that He is ever-present in the waters of life and during the fiery trials of life. As seen in Proverbs 15:3, "the eyes of the Lord are in every place, keeping watch on the evil and the good." Realizing this great truth, the Psalmist proclaims:

O Lord, you have searched me [thoroughly] and have known me. You know when I sit down and when I rise [my entire life, everything I do]; You understand my thoughts from afar.

You scrutinize my path and my lying down, And You are intimately acquainted with all my ways. Even before there is a word on my tongue [still unspoken], Behold, O Lord - You know it all. You have enclosed me behind and before, and [You have] placed Your hand upon me. Such [infinite] knowledge is too wonderful for me; It is too high [above me],

---

[87] Jeremiah 23:24 - English Standard Version (ESV).

I cannot reach it.[88]

So, the good news is, the boundless Master Builder is ever-present in every season of life.

There are no happenings in the marketplace, no world events, or spiritual heights that can hinder God's presence. In reference to humans, Tozer declares:

> *The doctrine of the divine omnipresence personalizes [humans'] relation to the universe in which [they find themselves]. This great central truth gives meaning to all truths and imparts supreme value to [every aspect of humans'] life. God is present, near [humans], next to [humans], and this God sees [humans]and knows [humans] through and thorough.*[89]

The infinite God who knows us through and thorough, desires for humans to enter a covenant relationship with Him.

The Bible reveals precise instructions for entering a covenant relationship with God. For instance, coupled with belief in His existence, the starting point of everyone's relationship with God

---

[88] Psalm 139:1-6 - Amplified Bible (AMP).

[89] Tozer 88

is the use of faith. By faith, diligent seekers accept the Master Builder's threefold invitation: to rest in Him, to follow Him, and to build with Him. At the point of acceptance, true believers yoke up with the Master Builder.

Yoking up with the Master Builder means the Christian has entered a partnership with the Lord Jesus Christ. The partnership requires faithfulness from God as well as the Christian. Without fail, God is eternally faithful! However, Spirit-filled believers must prove their faithfulness by consistently adhering to five major principles: 1) seeking God first, 2) trusting the Lord wholeheartedly, 3) always acknowledging the Lord, 4) glorifying God in every dimension of wealth, and 5) remembering the infinite Master Builder is the source of wealth.

When Christians adhere to God's principles for building wealth, the Master Builder gives guidance. He orders our steps in the plain path of righteousness. Although the path of righteousness may lead to challenging circumstances, Christians must trust in the Lord. Even when God leads Christians into the valleys and storms of life, we must:

> *Trust in the Lord with all* [our] *heart, and do not lean on* [our] *own understanding. In all* [our] *ways* [we must] *acknowledge*

Gwen E. Brannum

Him. . .[90]

When Christians trust and acknowledge the Master Builder, He faithfully fulfills His part by making our "paths straight and smooth - removing obstacles that block [our] way."[91]

In addition to directing the paths of His people, the Lord faithfully counsels and instructs Christians. When true believers respond to God in faith-filled obedience, they prosper both spiritually and naturally. God is known for rewarding individuals who respond to Him in faith. In fact, the Bible gives extraordinary examples of individuals who obtained the promises of God by faithfully following His plan and purposes.

The lives of Abraham, Isaac, and Jacob are splendid examples of how God rewards faith-filled obedience. Other notable examples are the Reubenites, Gadites, and the half-tribe of Manasseh. Joshua reminded them of their obedience by saying:

. . .you have kept all that Moses the servant of the LORD commanded you and have listened to and obeyed my voice

---

[90] Proverbs 3:5-6 - King James Version (KJV).

[91] Proverbs 3:6 - Amplified Bible (AMP).

50

in everything that I commanded you.[92]

As a result, "the Lord [their] God [gave] rest to [their] brothers, as He had promised them. . ."[93] In addition to blessing their brothers, God also blessed the individuals who initiated the blessing through their faith-filled obedience.

God knows when and how to give wealthy portions of what He owns. For example,

> *When Joshua sent the Reubenites and the Gadites and the half-tribe of Manasseh away to their tents, he blessed them, and he said to them, return to your tents with great riches and with very many livestock, with silver, gold, bronze, iron, and with very many clothes. . .*[94]

The first thing on the list is great riches. Next, the list reveals a bountiful supply of wealth given to the men so they can "live and flourish as human beings created in the image of God,"[95] The entire story seen in the twenty-second chapter of Joshua serves as a

---

[92] Joshua 22:2 - Amplified Bible (AMP).

[93] Joshua 22:4 - Amplified Bible (AMP).

[94] Joshua 22:7 & 8 - Amplified Bible (AMP).

[95] For the Least of These (pp. 60-61). Zondervan Academic. Kindle Edition.

testimony of how God's people prosper through faith filled obedience.

Learning from the Reubenites, Gadites, and the half-tribe of Manasseh, marketplace Christians can respond to God's Word in faith-filled obedience and receive God's conditional promises. Interestingly, God fulfills His unconditional promises despite the actions of humans. However, to reap the conditional promises of God, believers must satisfy the requirements He has set. For example, believers can receive godly wisdom when they meet God's requirement of asking in faith. James 1:5-7 states:

> *If any of you lacks wisdom, you should ask God, who gives generously to all without finding fault, and it will be given to you. But when you ask, you must believe and not doubt, because the one who doubts is like a wave of the sea, blown and tossed by the wind. That person should not expect to receive anything from the Lord.*[96]

On the other hand, the person who satisfies God with faith will receive godly wisdom.

In the workplace, the wisdom of God is necessary for

---

[96] James 1:5-7 - New International Version (NIV).

making choices that will glorify God in our daily business transactions. The wisdom of God is also necessary for making decisions that will honor God during interactions between colleagues. In addition, God's wisdom will help Christians discern the right career path. Whatever the case may be, Christians can simply:

> *Pray to the Father. He loves to help.* [We will] *get His help, and* [will not] *be condescended to when* [we] *ask for* [wisdom]. [When we] *ask boldly, believingly, without a second thought* [we will receive godly wisdom].

By God's design, anyone who follows the divine instructions seen in James 1:5-7 coupled with Hebrews 11:6 will receive the conditional promises of God.

In addition to giving wisdom during seasons of trials and temptations, God constantly fulfills His promises in the lives of faith-filled followers. In fact, every Christian has already received great and precious promises from God. According to 2 Peter 1:3-4:

> *[God's] divine power has given us everything we need for a godly life through our knowledge of Him who called us by His own glory and goodness. Through these He has given us His very great and precious promises, so that through them [we] may participate in the divine nature, having escaped*

the corruption in the world caused by evil desires.[97]

Through the wisdom of God that has been revealed in Christ Jesus, Christians can live victoriously in every season of life.

By God's design, there will be pleasant as well as unpleasant seasons on the path of enduring wealth. Unpleasant seasons are unavoidable. The Bible informs, "The good [person] does not escape all troubles – [he or she] has them too. . ."[98] So, marketplace Christians will inevitably encounter challenging times in the workplace as well as other aspects of life.

Nevertheless, believers must exercise faith in God. Exercising faith gives the believer an opportunity to watch God at work as He demonstrates His infinite wisdom on the behalf of the believer. As stated by Tozer, "The testimony of faith is that - no matter how things look in this fallen world, all God's acts are wrought in perfect wisdom."[99] Whatever the Master Builder allows believers to encounter is based on His infinite wisdom in effort to reveal His glory, give insight, and prosper His people in every

---

[97] 2 Peter 1:4 - The Voice (VOICE).

[98] Psalm 34:19 - Living Bible (TLB).

[99] Tozer 73

season of life.

If Christian workers desire to glorify God in every sphere of the marketplace, we must exude faith. Tozer declares:

> *it is vitally important that we hold the truth of God's infinite wisdom as a tenet of our creed; but this is not enough. We must, by the exercise of faith and by prayer, bring it into the practical world of our day-by-day experience.* [100]

Every day, in every area of life, Christians must trust the wisdom of God.

Christians who hold the truth of God's infinite wisdom as the foundation of their belief, they walk by faith and not by sight. When pleasant seasons transition into unpleasant seasons, true believers have bold confidence in God. In every season, faith-filled followers hold on to the truth reveal in 1 Corinthians 10:13:

> *God is faithful, and He will not let* [us] *be tempted beyond* [our] *ability, but with the temptation He will also provide the way of escape, that* [we] *may be able to endure it.* [101]

Christians can rejoice because challenging seasons are not designed

---

[100] Tozer 74

[101] 1 Corinthians 10:13 - New International Version (NIV).

to cause faith-filled followers to be defeated.

However, God allows Christians to encounter unpleasant situations so they can see the reality of Romans 5:3-5:

> . . .*tribulation worketh patience; and patience, experience; and experience, hope: and hope maketh not ashamed; because the love of God is shed abroad in our hearts by the Holy Ghost which is given unto us.*[102]

Even during tribulations, Christians have an opportunity to increase in spiritual wealth.

With the spiritual increase of patience, experience, and hope, Christians are fortified to practice spiritual discipline. Two spiritual disciplines that come to mind are studying the Bible and praying. Through the spiritual discipline of studying God's Word, Christians gain a greater understanding of the importance of trusting God. In addition, through the discipline of prayer, Christians receive illumination. During prayer, Christians also become more acquainted with the infinite Master Builder who is the only constant source of unshakable strength.

Through the unshakeable strength of God, Christian workers

---

[102] Romans 5:3-5 - King James Version (KJV).

can glorify God in every sphere of the marketplace. Despite the unstable infrastructure of the marketplace, Christians can still glorify God because they are thoroughly convinced - God is faithful. Great and beyond measure is His faithfulness.[103] Without fail, God knows the exact time to allow His people to see His salvation.

In His infinite wisdom, God faithfully changes the seasons of life at the appointed time. As a result, marketplace Christians see the faithfulness of God as He shows Himself strong on their behalf. By showing Himself strong in the workplace is a clear indication that the Master Builder approves work. Amazingly, from the beginning of time, God elevates the theme of work.

As seen in the Bible, the infinite Creator of the universe elected to introduce Himself at work. He demonstrated the value of work for six days before resting on the seventh day. Starting in Genesis, He promotes the theme of work as honorable, essential, and right. The boundless Master Builder could have completed all His creation in an instance. Instead, He chose to demonstrate the high qualities and nature of work.

The Builder and Maker of all things presents work as a desirable quality that humans should perform in the spirit of

---

[103] Lamentations 3:23 - Amplified Bible (AMP).

excellence. In addition, the Master Builder reveals He is a God of order. From the grandest galaxy to the smallest mammal, all creation flows harmoniously in the exact order God intended. By God's design, every star musically twinkles in a specific order.

In addition to governing the stars, the master Builder governs when and how the earth rotates. Without becoming exasperated or exhausted, the Builder and Maker of all things governs the rotation of the earth. Amicably, just as the Master Builder intended, the planet Earth never misses a spin around its own axis. Never in reverse, spinning from the west to the east, planet Earth constantly spins counterclockwise.

As planet Earth spins toward the east, agreeably, the sun, the moon, and the stars rise in the east. Setting in the west - the stars, the moon, and the sun amicably bow to the Master Builder's intended purpose. Without hindrance, in every season of life, God's intended purpose is unfolding. Even unpleasant seasons draped in defeat gives way to God's intended purpose. For example, when the past dispensations closed in judgement, God's plan continued to unfold in a new dispensation.

Every new dispensation represents the unhindered plan of God. In addition, within the span of time allotted for each dispensation, God reveals His glory, gives insight, and prospers His people. All day, every day, God is revealing His glory in creation.

So much so, in every country throughout the world, "the heavens are telling of the glory of God; and the expanse [of heaven] is declaring the work of His hands."[104] Although the heavens declare the glory of the infinite Master Builder, the intricate details of His works are incomprehensible.

---

[104] Psalm 19:1 - Amplified Bible (AMP).

Chapter 3

The Master Builder's

Incomprehensible Works

No one will ever be able to fully explain the Master Builder's creative techniques. Every facet of His majestic construction is incomprehensible. Even the best scientific effort to explain the creation of the universe proves to be imperfect to say the least. Mainly because a hypothesis is:

> *a manufactured construct that [tries] to make sense of God's creation using finite, fallen reason. Such a theory is not only fallible, but it can at best [supply] a model of a contingent, temporal reality.*[105]

Temporal realities constructed by finite reasoning will never reveal the infinite Master Builder's creation secrets.

Although the intricate details of God's building secrets are beyond finite understanding, by faith Christians are convinced, God is the Builder and Maker of the heavens and the earth. In other words:

---

[105] A Theology for all Seasons on the 500th Anniversary of the Reformation (pp. 220-221).

> *By faith [that is, with an inherent trust and enduring confidence in the power, wisdom and goodness of God] we understand that the worlds (universe, ages) were framed and created [formed, put in order, and equipped for their intended purpose] by the word of God, so that what is seen was not made of things which are visible.* [106]

Without the type of faith that is seen in Hebrews 11:3, humans' finite minds do not have the capacity to understand that the universe was made by the word of God.

Furthermore, without faith, the finite mind cannot comprehend how all space, time, and matter exist in the eternal mind of God. Just trying to grasp the concept of God eternally knowing how the skies would display His artistry is overwhelming. Adding to the astonishment, the Bible reveals before "the celestial realms announced [His] glory"[107] the Master Builder declared ". . .the end from the beginning, and from ancient times the things that are not yet done. . ."[108] So, God eternally knows the precise details of every season and purpose under the sun.

Before the Master Builder called the sun into existence, He

---

[106] Hebrews 11:3 - Amplified Bible (AMP).

[107] Psalm 19:1 - The Voice Bible (VOICE)).

[108] Isaiah 46:10 - King James Version (KJV).

purposed to display His glory in every season. In fact, before He spoke space, time, or the seraphim into existence, He purposed for the heavens to declare His glory and for the firmament to show His handiwork.[109] Amazingly, He even purposed for the seraphim to call one to another, "Holy, holy, holy is the Lord Almighty; the whole earth is full of His glory."[110] All of God's creation was designed to declare His glory.

For His glory, the Master Builder spoke particles, compounds, and complex cells into existence. Not one phase of creation took place outside of God's plan. According to the counsel of His own will, the Master Builder designed all things. Colossians 1:16 declares:

> It was by Him that everything was created: the heavens, the earth, all things within and upon them, all things seen and unseen, thrones and dominions, spiritual powers, and authorities. Every detail was crafted through His design, by His own hands, and for His purposes.[111]

Therefore, as seen in Genesis 1:1, "In the beginning God [intentionally with a divine purpose] created the heavens and the

---

[109] Psalm 19:1 - King James Version (KJV).

[110] Isaiah 6:2-3 - New International Version (NIV).

[111] Colossians 1:16 - The Voice (VOICE).

earth."[112]

Creating the heavens and earth was no mystery to God. The omniscient Master Builder knew precisely how to make the heavens and the earth. Without anyone's opinion, He simply spoke, and it was so. Unlike finite builders, the omniscient Master Builder did not need an architect, or engineer, or surveyor because God's architectural design is infallible. Implementing His detailed plan required no masonry tools, construction machines, power drills, hammers, or nails. The only tool the Master Builder used was - His spoken Word. Psalm 33:9 declares: "When He spoke, the world began! It appeared at His command."

Any time the Master Builder speaks, amazing things happen. For example, on the first day, "God said, "Let there be light;" and there was light."[113] Genesis 1:4-5 declares:

> God saw that the light was good (pleasing, useful) and He affirmed and sustained it; and God separated the light [distinguishing it] from the darkness. And God called the light day, and the darkness He called night. And there was evening and there was morning, one day. [114]

---

[112] Genesis 1:1 - Darby Translation (DARBY).

[113] Genesis 1:3 - Amplified Bible (AMP).

[114] Genesis 1:4-5 - Amplified Bible (AMP).

Genesis 1:7-8 reveals, on the second day, the Master Builder said:

> *Let there be an expanse* [amid] *the waters, and let it be a division between waters and waters. And God made the expanse and divided between the waters that are under the expanse and the waters that are above the expanse; and it was so. And God called the expanse Heavens. And there was evening, and there was morning—a second day.*[115]

So far, there is light, water, and the heavens. But where are the sun, moon, and stars? Remember, the Master Builder eternally purposed to speak His creation into existence – in a precise order.

Step by step, God revealed His infallible plan. In His own suitable time, after God named the dry land "earth," and the water "seas,"[116] He said:

> *Let the earth burst forth with every sort of grass and seed-bearing plant, and fruit trees with seeds inside the fruit, so that these seeds will produce the kinds of plants and fruits they came from." And so it was, and God was pleased. This all occurred on the third day.*[117]

At this point, it is worth noting that the third day is of great

---

[115] Genesis 1:7-8 - Darby Translation (DARBY).

[116] Genesis 1:10 - Living Bible (TLB).

[117] Genesis 1:11 - English Standard Version (ESV).

significance. In fact, every time "the third day"[118] is mentioned in the Bible, the incomprehensible works of God are highlighted.

Reflecting on the first three days of creation, each day, adds an immeasurable exclamation mark to the incomprehensible works of the Master Builder. Notice, on the first day God created light but there is no mentioning of the sun, moon, and stars. With that thought in mind, the first three days close without the sun ruling by day and the moon ruling by night. Therefore, on the third day, the vegetation, plants yielding seed, and fruit trees grew out of the earth without any help from the sun. However, according to the Master Builder's blueprint, the sun, the moon, and the stars were destined to fulfill their intended purposes.

Just as God planned, on the fourth day the Master Builder said:

Let there be lights in the sky. These lights will separate the days from the nights. They will be used for signs to show when special meetings begin and to show the days and years. They will be in the sky to shine light on the earth. And it happened. So, God made the two large lights. He made the

---

[118] Reference "the third day": Genesis 22:4-8, Exodus 19:16-25, Leviticus 19:5-8, Numbers 7:24-29, Hosea 6:1-3, Matthew 15:32-39, Matthew 17:22-23, John 2:1-5, John 19:1-3, Luke 24:7, and Luke 24:46.

larger light to rule during the day and the smaller light to rule during the night. He also made the stars.[119]

Even the stars are held firmly in place at the command of the Master Builder. In fact, before the creation, "He decided how many stars there would be in the sky and gave each one a name."[120]

All because of the sustaining power of the "Father of lights," the stars still exist. To expand our thinking, He left on record in Isaiah 40:26:

Lift your eyes and look to the heavens: Who created all these? He who brings out the starry host one by one and calls forth each of them by name. Because of His great power and mighty strength, not one of them is missing.[121]

The same Creator and Sustainer of the starry host is the One who predetermined every phase of creation. He had a set order for speaking His masterpiece into existence. Therefore, not one solitary star, plant, animal, fish of the sea, or fowl of the air slipped up on the scene prematurely.

Further observation of the Scriptures reveals the Master Builder determined in eternity every facet of time, space, and matter.

---

[119] Genesis 1:14-16 - Easy-to-Read Version (ERV).

[120] Psalms 147:4 - Contemporary English Version (CEV).

[121] Isaiah 40:26 - New International Version (NIV).

Then, He demonstrated His thoughts in creation. Testifying about His own creative power, in Isaiah 45:12, the Master Builder said, "I made the earth and created man upon it. My hands stretched out the heavens, and I commanded all their host."[122] Therefore, God is responsible for all the mysterious beauty of creation. So, the universe, humans, living creatures, vegetation, plants yielding seed, and fruit trees bearing fruit did not happen by osmosis.

The Master Builder - intentionally spoke His detailed plan into existence. Unlike finite builders, God did not use existing resources to create the Universe. In other words, the Master Builder did not design the heavens and the earth with existing space and time. According to Don Stewart, "when God created the heavens and the earth, He also created space and time."[123] Psalm 33:9 declares:

[God] spoke, and all things [the heavens, the earth, space, and time] came into being. A single command from His lips,

---

[122] Isaiah 45:12 - Amplified Bible (AMP).

[123] What Was God Doing before He Created the Universe? by Don Steward - https://www.blueletterbible.org/faq/don_stewart/don_stewart_643.cfm - accessed March 2022.

and all creation obeyed and stood its ground.[124]

Since God created everything, He knows how every facet of time and space will be used.

God knows the precise amount of space that exist between the planets. He knows the exact amount of space and time that is needed for "planet earth" to spin on its axis - causing day and night. In His infinite wisdom, the Master Builder uses space and time as He tilts an entire world at a perfect angle causing the seasons to change. For instance, the US Department of Commerce, National Oceanic and Atmospheric Administration, as well as the National Weather Service inform:

> *the earth's spin axis [tilts] with respect to its orbital plane. This is what causes the seasons. When the earth's axis points towards the sun, it is summer for that hemisphere. When the earth's axis points away, [winter is coming]. For the Northern Hemisphere, the axis points most toward the sun in June (specifically around June 21) and away from the sun around December 21. This corresponds to the Winter and Summer Solstice (solstice is Latin for "the sun stands").*[125]

---

[124] Psalm 33:9 - The Voice Bible (VOICE)).

[125] https://www.weather.gov/lmk/seasons.

In addition to Winter and Summer, by God's design, "there is a season (a time appointed) for everything and a time for every delight and event or purpose under heaven."[126] Ecclesiastes reveals a vivid picture of life's seasons: times of birth, death, weeping, and laughing. In addition, Ecclesiastes confirms the fact that everyone will experience good and unpleasant seasons throughout their life span. But in every season of life, the Master Builder instructs us to "be still in the presence of the Lord and wait patiently for Him to act."[127] His action plan is to reveal His glory, give insight, prosper His people, and give peace in every season.

Despite the atrocities, diseases, and disappointments of life, Christians can experience the peace of God. Unlike worldly comfort and happiness, God's peace guards the hearts and minds of believers during trials and sorrows. Notice what the Prince of Peace reveals in John 16:33, '. . . here on earth you will have trials and sorrows. But take heart because I have overcome the world."[128]

The One who has overcome the world provides incomprehensible peace. He is also the One who created the seasons

---

[126] Ecclesiastes 3:1a - Amplified Bible (AMP).

[127] Psalms 37:7 - New Living Translation (NLT).

[128] John 16: 33 - New Living Translation (NLT).

of life. In His infinite wisdom, God allows His people to encounter pleasant as well as unpleasant seasons. Even the disciples who closely followed Jesus experienced different seasons in life. Can you imagine having a season of following the Master Teacher and suddenly following Him in person is no longer a possibility?

Just imagine the Master Teacher informing you, "a time is coming and in fact has come when you will [scatter], each to your own home. You will leave me all alone."[129] To me, that is a huge change in season. But being the Prince of Peace, He quickly offers comfort by saying, "I have told you these things, so that in Me you may have peace."[130]

The peace that Jesus gives - is an incomprehensible gift from God. Despite the adverse happenings of the marketplace, Christian workers can enjoy the gift of God's peace. For example, during a foundational shift, Christian product managers can cast their cares upon the Lord and experience peace. Even when the best customer-focused efforts do not produce a bottom-line profit, Christian owners can still experience peace. Why? Because the Master Builder who is the Prince of Peace is available to give peace to all who cast their

---

[129] John 16:32 - New International Version (NIV).

[130] John 16:33a - New International Version (NIV).

cares upon Him.

Apostle Paul experienced the unfathomable peace of God. He also wanted other believers to experience God's peace. So much so, He encourages them in Philippians 4:6-7 by saying:

> [Do not] *worry over anything whatever; tell God every detail of your needs in earnest and thankful prayer, and the peace of God which transcends human understanding, will keep constant guard over your hearts and minds as they rest in Christ Jesus.*[131]

Resting in the Lord, Christians enjoy the benefits of God's peace. For instance, the peace of God empowers Christians to face the challenges of the marketplace with a godly composure. Also, as the peace of God guards the hearts and minds of Christians, they gain greater insight concerning the unavoidable seasons of life.

Amidst the inevitable seasons of life, Apostle Paul learned how to be content in any and every circumstance. Being yoked up with the Master Teacher, Paul learned the secret to facing every season. In fact, Apostle Paul declares in Philippians 4:12-13:

> *I know how to get along and live humbly in* [challenging times]*, and I also know how to enjoy abundance and live in prosperity. In any and every circumstance I have learned the*

---

[131] Philippians 4:6-7 - J.B. Phillips New Testament (PHILLIPS).

secret [of facing life], whether well-fed or going hungry, whether having an abundance, or being in need. I can do all things [which He has called me to do] through Him who strengthens and empowers me [to fulfill His purpose—I am self-sufficient in Christ's sufficiency; I am ready for anything and equal to anything through Him who infuses me with inner strength and confident peace.][132]

Like Apostle Paul, every Christian must learn how to rely on the strength of God in every season of life.

Seasons are an inseparable part of the infinite Master Builder's incomprehensible works. As seen in Genesis 8:22, "as long as the earth endures, seedtime and harvest, cold and heat, summer and winter, day and night will never cease."[133] In addition to ordaining the seasons in nature, God has ordained various seasons for humans on a personal level. So, by God's design, all Christian workers will experience good as well as unpleasant seasons.

Despite the unpleasant seasons of life, God is at work. Ecclesiastes 3:11 reveals:

He has made everything beautiful in its time. He has also set eternity in the human heart; yet no one can fathom what God

---

[132] Philippians 4:12-13 - Amplified Bible (AMP).

[133] Genesis 8:22 - New International Version (NIV).

has done from beginning to end.[134]

Although humans cannot comprehend the intricate details of what the Master Builder has done from beginning to end, Christians can praise God for His faithfulness.

Because of the faithfulness of God, Spirit-filled believers can say like Isaiah:

> *Lord, you are my God; I will exalt You and praise Your name, for in perfect faithfulness You have done wonderful things, things planned long ago.*[135]

Before the foundation of the world, God planned to prosper His people in every season of life. The ending of one season and the start of a new season can prove to be a form of prosperity. For instance, when a Christian worker transitions out of an unpleasant season to a pleasant season, he or she prospers by gaining another testimony of victory.

Having testimonies of victorious outcomes assist with equipping marketplace Christians to be effective witnesses. Victorious testimonies are the product of pleasant as well as unpleasant seasons. Interestingly, history reveals that powerful

---

[134] Ecclesiastes 3:11- New International Version (NIV).

[135] Isaiah 25:1- New International Version (NIV).

testimonies that develop during unpleasant seasons can have a profound impact. History also reveals there are testimonies that are so powerful they change the trajectory of lives all over the world. Other powerful testimonies inspire the creation of songs and books. In any given case, the Master Builder works in seasons to reveal His glory, give insight, and prosper His people.

Despite the seasons of life and the happenings of the marketplace, God faithfully unfolds His plan. As God unfolds His plan, He allows marketplace workers to go from one season to another season. During the change of every season, the Master Builder reveals His glory, gives insight, and prospers His people. For example, an entrepreneur can start out enthusiastically working, excelling, and securing one contract after another. But in God's infinite wisdom, He transitions the same prosperous entrepreneur into a season where there is a decline in business transactions. Although the entrepreneur may swiftly transition into what he or she perceives to be an unpleasant season, the Master Builder is still at work.

In unpleasant seasons, the Lord gives entrepreneurs an opportunity to use their faith in an unfamiliar area of life. During unusual times, Christians must remember the words of the Psalmist, "many hardships and perplexing circumstances confront the righteous, but the Lord rescues him [or her] from them all."[136]

---

[136] Psalm 34:19 - Amplified Bible (AMP).

Christians must also remember, the One who delivers all His faith-filled followers said, ". . .take heart because I have overcome the world. . ."[137] With that thought in mind, Christian workers have hope because the Master Builder who has overcome the world knows how and when to change the seasons of life.

Like seasons, God has also woven time into the fabric of life. According to the King James Version Dictionary, time is "a particular portion or part of duration, whether past, present or future."[138] Adding greater insight, Holman Bible Dictionary states, time is "the chronological sequence of life and its significance in biblical teachings."[139] By creating the universe, the Master Builder set the stage for His eternal plan to unfold in time.

Life as we know it, is inseparable from time. Every event has a duration of time used for God's plan and purposes. Throughout the Bible, in every dispensation, God works within time to reveal different facets of His wealth-building blueprint. The entire Bible supplies great insight into how the Master Builder works in time as He governs the affairs of His creation. However, due to the boundless nature of God, He transcends every facet of time and

---

[137] John 16: 33 - New Living Translation (NLT).

[138] Online dictionary of King James Version – accessed May 2022.

[139] https://www.studylight.org/dictionaries/eng/hbd/t/time-meaning-of.html - accessed March 2022.

every season.

Having transcendence over all His creation, the Master Builder knows how, why, and when to change the times and the seasons.[140] In His acts of creation, God demonstrates His transcendence over time as He set up the sequence of days, nights, seasons, and years. For example, in Genesis 1:14:

> *God said, let there be lights in the firmament of the heaven to divide the day from the night; and let them be for signs, and for seasons, and for days, and years.*[141]

Speaking of days and years, Psalm 90:4 states, "a thousand years in [the boundless Master Builder's] sight is but as yesterday when it is past, and as a watch in the night" [142] because He is sovereign. In every dispensation, God proves His sovereignty as He paces world events to unfold His eternal plan.

Being the Supreme Ruler, God eternally knows the chronological order for every event under the sun. There has never been anything that took place in the marketplace or anywhere else without His knowledge. Just as He has always known the exact date the Law would be wrote on the table of stones; He also has always

---

[140] Daniel 2:21 – King James Version (KJV).

[141] Genesis 1:14 - King James Version (KJV).

[142] Psalm 90:4 – King James Version (KJV).

known the exact date "Gutenberg Printing Press" would print the first article. In addition, the Master Builder has always known the precise time the "Industrial and Technological Revolution" would happen. Not only has He eternally known about Gutenberg Printing Press and the millions of other businesses, but the Master Builder owns the entire marketplace.

The Bible emphatically states, "the earth is the Lord's, and the fulness thereof; the world, and they that dwell therein."[143] Furthermore, the Master Builder left on record in Haggai 2:6, "the silver is mine, and the gold is mine."[144] Not only does He owns the silver and gold, but He freely gives wealth and riches to those who will faithfully follow His plan. Notice what He said in Isaiah 45:3-4:

> *I will give you riches hidden in the darkness and things of great worth that are hidden in secret places. Then you may know that it is I, the Lord, the God of Israel, who calls you by name. For the good of Jacob My servant and Israel My chosen one, I called you by your name. I gave you a name of honor when you had not known Me.*[145]

---

[143] Psalm 24:1 - King James Version (KJV).

[144] Haggai 2:8 – Kings James Version (KJV).

[145] Isaiah 45:3 – New Life Version (NLV).

Although God was speaking about the king of Persia in Isaiah 45:3-4, it is worth noting that Cyrus received riches because God was unfolding His plan. While the king of Persia was oblivious of Isaiah's prophecy, God's plan was progressively unfolding. From start to finish, God demonstrates His sovereignty as He allows Cyrus' season of reigning to coincide with the Israelites' season of exile. God eternally purposed for Cyrus to reign before his mother conceived him. Before the birth of Cyrus, Isaiah prophesied that the king of Persia would be Cyrus.

The God-breathed prophecy happened according to God's timing. Not only did Cyrus kingship happen according to God's timing, but, at the appointed time, Cyrus overthrew the powerful monarchy of the Persian Empire. Now remember, Cyrus is oblivious to the fact that he is fulfilling the plan of God. But, by divine order, after Cyrus invaded Persia, Daniel who carefully studied the scroll of Jeremiah, realized that the Israelites' 70 years of captivity has ended. Daniel also realized that God was unfolding an astonishing prophecy concerning the invasion of Persia.

Based on the Scriptures, Daniel knew that Cyrus was the King who God chose to liberate the Israelites from exile. So, Daniel showed the scroll to Cyrus. However, being oblivious to the plan of God, Cyrus looked shocked to see his name recorded in the Scriptures. Nevertheless, Cyrus gained the necessary confidence to follow the plan of God. By the divine order of God, Cyrus liberated the Jews from their exile. As the prophecy continued to unfold, Cyrus returned the Jews to the land of Israel and issued a decree authorizing the Jews to rebuild Solomon's Temple.

After Cyrus issued a decree authorizing the Jews to rebuild the Temple, God fulfilled His promise. In due season, God gave Cyrus "riches hidden in the darkness and things of great worth that [were] hidden in secret places."[146] Even the revealing of the treasures happened like clockwork. When Cyrus fulfilled the plan of God, something wonderful took place. For example, God guided Cyrus' soldiers who were in Babylon to unearthed substantial amounts of gold and silver. Why? Because God is faithful, and He keeps His promises. Whatever He has spoken He will fulfill it.[147]

The faithful Master Builder who fulfills His promises, led Cyrus' soldiers to the hidden treasures under the Euphrates River. Although the king of Babylon securely hid the treasures, the all-knowing King of kings knew the exact location. Even though the king of Babylon was placing the wealth under the Euphrates River for future use, the King of kings had a bigger plan in mind. While unfolding His plan, the Master Builder faithfully oversaw the affairs of both the Persia empire as well as the Babylonian empire. Being King of kings, He timed the affairs of earthly kingdoms to reveal

---

[146] Isaiah 45:3 – New Life Version (NLV).

[147] Numbers 23:19 – King James Version (KJV).

His glory.

For His glory, God gave insight to Daniel, Cyrus, and the Israelites. Watch the astonishing process. First, God gave Isaiah insight concerning the upcoming king of Persia. Centuries later, He gave Daniel insight to understand that Isaiah's prophecy was unfolding according to the divine order of God. The Jews' 70 years of exile was over, and the king of Persia is Cyrus. Now the stage is set for Daniel to tell Cyrus about his role in God's plan for liberating the Jews. Having the necessary insight, Cyrus followed the plan and returned the Jews to their homeland.

In the process of their liberation from exile, the Jews gained greater insight concerning the sovereign God of the universe. God revealed greater aspects of His character to the Jews by allowing them to experience the fulfillment of His promise. After being delivered, the Israelites realized, "[God alone knows] the plans [He has for His people] . . . plans to prosper [them] and not to harm [them], plans to give [them] hope and a future."[148] Although the Israelites may have thought their season of being in exile was far too long, God was pacing the end of their season with Cyrus' season of being king. God is still in the business of ordering the steps of His

---

[148] Jeremiah 29:11 - New International Version (NIV).

people to bring about His plan.

From the day of one's birth God governs the events of his or her life. Although God created humans with a free will to make choices in life, He has a precise plan for each human. On a larger scale, His overall plan is for humans to revere Him and keep His commandments. In addition, He plans to prosper believers who faithfully adhere to His blueprint. Also, He gives all faith-filled followers greater insight, a wealth of peace, and prosperity in every season of life.

There are people who cannot perceive the idea of experiencing a wealth of peace and prosperity in every season. Nevertheless, the Prince of Peace knows how to saturate the hearts and minds of His people with peace "which transcends all understanding."[149] The peace of God gives Christians the necessary mental stability and spiritual equilibrium to keep their minds on Him. The key to maintaining and enjoying the perfect peace of God is keeping our minds focused on Him. When Christians focus on the Prince of Peace, they learn more about how He works to prosper His people.

Currently, God is available to release His peace in every

---

[149] Philippians 4:7 - New International Version (NIV).

sphere of the marketplace. He is at work revealing His glory, giving insight, and prospering marketplace Christians. The boundless Master Builder who is at work within Christian workers can do "infinitely beyond their highest prayers, desires, thoughts, or hopes."[150] Since God is at work within marketplace Christians, it is essential for us to yield to His will. Yielding to God's will is a demonstration of faith. Another demonstration of faith is to seek God first in every season of life. Seeking God first also prevents Christians from immediately leaning to their own understanding.

Furthermore, seeking God first is essential for staying on the path of enduring wealth. As a matter of fact, the Master Builder's blueprint informs believers to, "seek His will in all [we] do, [because] He takes the guess work out of life and He [shows believers] which path to take."[151] Since He knows all the paths in life, the boundless Master Builder knows how to lead and guide His people to wealthy places. He also knows how to lead His people away from the depraved deserts of life. In addition, the Master Builder knows how to bring unbelievers out of the valley of spiritual poverty.

Regardless of an individual's spiritual or natural situation, the Master Builder is a very present help for all who want to travel

---

[150] Ephesians 3:20 - Living Bible (TLB).

[151] Proverbs 3:6 - New Living Translation (NLT).

the path of enduring wealth. There is no valley low enough to keep the boundless Master Builder from helping all those who seek Him. Since He is boundless, He exists everywhere unhindered by the oppositions of life. So, despite the swift transitions of the marketplace, the boundless Master Builder knows how to faithfully deliver everyone who trusts and acknowledges Him.

When humans trust and acknowledge the Master Builder, He reveals His plan to prosper them in every dimension of wealth. He does not desire to see humans restlessly toil to build wealth. The Master Builder knows building wealth without His help is a daunting task. Therefore, He is willing and able to show all board members, shareholders, corporate officers, executive officers, and employees on all levels His blueprint for building wealth. But first, marketplace workers must believe that He exists and "that He cares enough to respond to those who seek Him."[152]

Every time the Master Builder responds to diligent seekers, He does it to reveal His glory, give insight, and place them on the path of enduring wealth. Even after seekers become faithful followers, the Master Builder keeps on revealing more of Himself. Why? Because God wants His people to know more about His thoughts and His ways. In every season of life, the Master Builder

---

[152] Hebrews 11:6 - The Message (MSG).

reveals greater aspects of His attributes by prospering His people. As surprising as it may be, sometimes God causes unbelievers to prosper so they can become acquainted with Him.

Remember, God prospered a king who was not a devout worshipper of the God of Israel. Although Cyrus was not serving God, he had an intricate roll in fulfilling the plan of God. As a result, God gave Cyrus great wealth. However, God was up to something greater than giving Cyrus earthly wealth. The boundless Master Builder was unfolding His plan to reveal Himself to Cyrus.

The Bible informs, God prospered Cyrus so he could "know that it is [God], the Lord, the God of Israel, who [called him] by name."[153] With that thought in mind, the same omniscient Master Builder who called Cyrus by name, has called every marketplace worker by name. Also, just as God had a precise purpose for Cyrus, He has a precise plan for every human. When humans submit to the plan of God, the boundless Master Builder reveals His glory, gives insight, and prospers His people in every season of life.

Despite the unavoidable seasons of life, the Master Builder leads His people in a plain path. While leading and prospering His people, the sovereign Master Builder is faithfully working to reveal

---

[153] Isaiah 45:3 – New Life Version (NLV).

His glory and give greater insight concerning who He is. However, it is important for Christians to remember, prosperity is not just tangible wealth but also spiritual wealth. Spiritual wealth comes by responding to the Master Builder's instructions in faith-filled obedience. At this very moment, He is instructing Christians, "lay not up for yourselves treasures upon earth. . . For where your treasure is, there will your heart be also." [154]

Adhering to the Master Builder's blueprint, faith-filled followers constantly focus on "[laying] up for [themselves] treasures in heaven, where neither moth nor rust doth corrupt, and where thieves do not break through nor steal."[155] C. H. Spurgeon explains:

> *Lay not out your life for gathering wealth: this would be degrading to you as servants of the heavenly kingdom. If you accumulate either money or raiment, your treasures will be liable to "moth and rust;" ... dishonest men may deprive you. That is an excellent reason for not making [earthly riches and wealth] the great objects of our pursuit. Hoard not for thieves, gather not for corruption: accumulate for eternity, and send your treasures into the land whither you*

---

[154] Matthew 6:19 & 21 - King James Version (KJV).

[155] Matthew 6:20 - King James Version (KJV).

are going. . .[156]

Christians who practice laying up treasures in heaven will increase in spiritual wealth. However, Christians who set their affections on earthly wealth will inevitably experience spiritual erosion.

The five warning signs of spiritual erosion are: 1) refusing to seek God first, 2) trusting your own abilities instead of trusting the Lord, 3) acknowledging everything and everybody except God, 4) failing to glorify God with your life, and 5) failing to reverence God for being the source of all wealth. The diagnosis for any of the five signs is a "carnal mind." Sadly, as seen in Romans 8:7: "the carnal mind is enmity against God: for it is not subject to the law of God, neither indeed can be."

To be clear, Romans 8:6 emphatically states, ". . . to be carnally minded is death; but to be spiritually minded is life and peace." Since life and peace are good and perfect gifts from

---

[156] https://www.preceptaustin.org/matthew_619-21.

[God],[157] they will never create spiritual erosion. Having life and peace, Christians are destined to prosper both spiritually and naturally. To consistently enjoy the benefits of having life and peace, Christians must adhere to the Master Builder's five wealth-building principles: 1) seeking God first in every season of life, 2) trusting the Lord wholeheartedly, 3) always acknowledging the Lord, 4) glorifying God in every dimension of wealth, and 5) remembering the infinite Master Builder is the source of all wealth.

Not only is God the source of all wealth, but He also freely gives wealth to all who obey and reverence Him. For example, while obeying and reverencing God, Adam and Eve prospered both spiritually and naturally. They had the ability to glorify God and have dominion over the earth. But through their disobedience, Adam and Eve lost their spiritual wealth.

Being catapulted into spiritual poverty, Adam and Eve lost

---

[157] James 1:17 – King James Version (KJV).

their fellowship with God. But due to the incomprehensible love of God, Adam and Eve were still allowed to live, move, and have their being[158] in the Eternal One. Because of God's mercy, Adam and Eve were blessed to "live and flourish as human beings created in the image of God."[159] In fact, the incomprehensible works of the Master Builder and His providential care were evident in the lives of Adam and Eve. For example, Genesis 3:21 reveals:

The Lord God used animal skins and made some clothes for the man and his wife. Then He put the clothes on them.[160]

There is a noticeable difference between the clothes that God made from animal skin verses the clothes that Adam and Eve made using fig leaves.

Ami Steinberger informs, "the Hebrew meaning for fig leaf

---

[158] Acts 17:28 - King James Version (KJV).

[159] For the Least of These (pp. 60-61). Zondervan Academic. Kindle Edition.

[160] Genesis 3:21 - Easy-to-Read Version (ERV).

is עֲלֵה תְאֵנָה both in the literal sense as well as in the sense borrowed from the biblical Garden of Eden account – a cover-up for something embarrassing."[161] In effort to cover-up their shame, Adam and Eve, "sewed fig leaves together and made coverings for themselves."[162] The clothes made from fig leaves were incapable of protecting humans from thorns and thistles. But God who is rich in mercy, provided adequate clothing for Adam and Eve.

Despite Adam and Eve being caught in the grip of spiritual poverty, God exercised His sovereignty and prospered them during the Conscience Dispensation. In fact, the boundless Master Builder is seen prospering His people in every dispensation.

---

[161] https://ulpan.com/how-to-say-fig-leaf-in-hebrew/

[162] Genesis 3:7 - New International Version (NIV).

Chapter 4

The Master Builder at Work in Every Dispensation

In the beginning, God set the stage to reveal His glory, give insight, and prosper His people in every dispensation. As the Dispensation of Innocence was coming into existence, the Master Builder worked six days and on the seventh day He rested. This is the same God who planned for humans to find rest in Christ Jesus. Resting in Christ Jesus is a spiritual realm where humans can experience the glory of God, receive insight, and prosper both spiritually and naturally.

The life of Adam and Eve presents a vivid picture of prospering according to the plan and purposes of God. Just as God planned, they were holy and wealthy. Their abundance of wealth begun with being fearfully and wonderfully made to reflect the image of God. Adam and Eve had perfect fellowship with God.

Since Adam and Eve were created on the sixth day, they had the privileged of being the first humans to enter God's rest on the seventh day. Resting in God and having dominion in the earth, Adam and Eve enjoyed both spiritual and natural prosperity. However, their spiritual prosperity ended abruptly when Adam and

Eve disobeyed God. Nevertheless, the unhindered plan of God continued to unfold. Despite the Fall of Adam, God is at work governing the affairs of humans for the sole purpose of revealing His glory, giving insight, and prospering His people.

As seen in the Bible, from the Dispensation of Conscience to the Dispensation of Grace, outside of Christ, humans are unholy, guilty, and restless. Based on the unholiness of humans, they struggle to build enduring wealth to no avail. Disregarding the Master Builder's blueprint, humans struggle to build their lives using devilish tools. Sadly, even in this Dispensation of Grace, humans are busy building without adhering to the Master Builder's plan.

Despite humans ignoring the Master Builder's blueprint, He is still unfolding His plan. In fact, after the Dispensation of Grace closes, the Master Builder will continue unfolding His plan during the Kingdom Age. The Kingdom Age, also called the Millennial Kingdom of Christ is the seventh dispensation. During the Kingdom age, the Master Builder will provide 1,000 years of rest. Notice, just as the Master Builder designed the seventh day of creation week as a day of rest, He also designed the seventh dispensation as a time of rest.

The Bible reveals the type of peace and rest humans will experience during the Millennial Kingdom of Christ. For example, Isaiah 32:17-18 states:

> *The fruit of that righteousness will be peace; its effect will*

be quietness and confidence forever. My people will live in peaceful dwelling places, in secure homes, in undisturbed places of rest.[163]

In addition to rest, there are five other important facts about the Millennial Kingdom of Christ: 1) Once again, there will be the physical presence of the Master Builder[164]; 2) a highway called the Way of Holiness shall be there[165]; 3) Satan will be bound in the Abyss[166]; 4) it will be a time of unity[167]; and 5) it will be a time of abundance.[168]

The abundance seen in the Millennial Kingdom of Christ is a reminder of the original plan that God had for humans. For example, during the Dispensation of Innocence, humans had the privilege of freely enjoying the abundance of God's provisions in peace. However, peacefully enjoying God's provisions requires faithful obedience to His commands. Just as God gave commands in

---

[163] Isaiah 32:17-18 - New International Version (NIV).

[164] Isaiah 16:5 - New King James Version (NKJV).

[165] Isaiah 35:8 - New King James Version (NKJV).

[166] Revelation 20:1–3 - New King James Version (NKJV).

[167] Isaiah 11:10 - New King James Version (NKJV).

[168] Isaiah 35:1–2 - New King James Version (NKJV).

the Dispensation of Innocence, He also gave precise commands applicable to the Dispensations of Conscience, Human Government, Promise, Law, and Grace. But due to humans' disobedience to God's commands, each dispensation ends in judgement. A summary of the dispensations:

Dispensation #1	Innocence Genesis 1:1 – Genesis 3:7	Transpired between the Creation and the Fall of Adam in the Garden
Dispensation #2	Conscience Genesis 3:8 - Genesis 8:22	Occurred between the Fall and the Flood
Dispensation #3	Human government Genesis 9:1 - Genesis 11:32	Transpired from the Flood to Abraham
Dispensation #4	Promise Genesis 12:1 - Exodus 19:25	Occurred from the time of Abraham to Moses
Dispensation #5	Law Exodus 20:1 – Acts 2:4	Occurred from the time of Moses to Jesus
Dispensation #6	The Age of Grace Acts 2:4 – Revelation 20:3	Took place from Pentecost to the Rapture—the Church Age
Dispensation #7	Millennial Kingdom Revelation 20:4-6	There will be 1000 Year Reign of Christ that begins with the 2nd Coming

Gwen E. Brannum

Speaking in terms of dispensations, the Bible does not explicitly teach dispensationalism. John Nelson Darby created premillennialism, which he called dispensationalism[169]. Darby viewed Bible history as a "progressive revelation, and his system sought to explain the stages in God's redemptive plan for the universe."[170] To me, Darby's system is an effective study tool for rightly dividing the Scriptures with guidance from the Holy Spirit. During prayerful study of God's Word, the Holy Spirit gives insight concerning the ways God collaborates with finite humans in every dispensation.

Working with Holy, Blameless, and Restful Humans

Before the restless state of humans, the omniscient Master Builder "formed man from the dust of the ground."[171] Amazingly,

---

[169] Christian History Magazine Editorial Staff. 131 Christians Everyone Should Know (Holman Reference) (p. 99). B&H Publishing Group. Kindle Edition.

[170] Christian History Magazine Editorial Staff. 131 Christians Everyone Should Know (Holman Reference) (p. 99). B&H Publishing Group. Kindle Edition.

[171] Genesis 2:7 - Amplified Bible, Classic Edition (AMP).

before He breathed His breath of life into the lifeless lump of clay, He knew all about the restless struggle humans would experience. Yet, He fulfilled His plans by creating humans to be holy, blameless, restful, and before Him in love. With that thought in mind, Christians can rejoice as they deeply ponder the truth of Ephesians 1:4-5:

> *Long ago, even before he made the world, God chose us to be his very own through what Christ would do for us; He decided then to make us holy in His eyes, without a single fault - we who stand before Him covered with His love. His unchanging plan has always been to adopt us into His own family by sending Jesus Christ to die for us. And He did this because He wanted to!*[172]

Humans exist to fulfill the eternal plan of God. In eternity, God planned to create humans for His glory and for His pleasure. Unfolding God's plan, the Master Builder, "created [humans], making them to be like Himself. He created them male and female."[173] Furthermore, God created humans to have fellowship with Him. Having communion with God is the catalyst for having

---

[172] Ephesians 1:4-5 - Living Bible (TLB).

[173] Genesis 1:27 - Good News Translation (GNT).

access to an abundance of wealth. Adam's communion with the Master Builder gave him direct access to a wealth of wisdom.

In addition to having direct access to a wealth of wisdom, Adam and Eve also had direct access to an abundance of knowledge and understanding. While helping to put the final addition on God's creation, Adam demonstrated a wealth of wisdom, knowledge, and understanding. For example, Genesis 2:19-20 reveals:

> . . .out of the ground the Lord God formed every [wild] beast and living creature of the field and every bird of the air and brought them to Adam to see what he would call them; and whatever Adam called every living creature, [that was their name]. And Adam gave names to all the livestock and to the birds of the air and to every [wild] beast of the field. . .[174]

Adam's fellowship with the Master Builder gave him access to God's blueprint for naming every living creature. By God's design, Adam demonstrated having dominion over all the earth. Just think, Adam and Eve were the first humans to experience the reality of Psalm 8:6-8. For instance, the Master Builder gave Adam and Eve:

> dominion over the works of [His] hands; [He] put all things

---

[174] Genesis 2:19-20 - Amplified Bible, Classic Edition (AMPC).

under [their] feet: all sheep and oxen, and the beasts of the field; The birds of the heavens, and the fish of the sea, and whatever passes through the paths of the seas.[175]

While having dominion during the Dispensation of Innocence, Adam and Eve had an opportunity to prove their obedience to the Master Builder's commands.

Adam and Eve received five commands: (1) replenish – the Hebrew verb is Mole meaning to fill, or make full the earth[176], (2) care for the garden, (3) subdue the earth, (4) have dominion over the animals, and (5) refrain from eating from the tree of knowledge of good and evil. Each of the commands depicts a vivid picture of the authority the Master Builder had bestowed upon humans. The commands served as God's authorization for Adam and Eve to freely use their wealth of wisdom, knowledge, and understanding. In fact, Adam and Eve had everything they needed to adhere to all the Master Builder's commands.

Not only were Adam and Eve endowed with a wealth of wisdom, knowledge, and understanding, but God endowed them

---

[175] Psalm 8:6-8 - Jubilee Bible 2000 (JUB).

[176] Smith, Joseph Fielding. Answers to Gospel Questions: Volumes 1-5. Deseret Book Company. Kindle Edition.

with freedom of choice. Having the freedom to choose, Adam and Eve could have refrained from eating from the tree of knowledge of good and evil. However, they ignored the warning:

> . . . *you must not eat from the tree that gives knowledge about good and evil. If you eat fruit from that tree, on that day you will certainly die!*[177]

Sadly, Adam and Eve died spiritually trying to increase their wealth of knowledge through disobedience.

Furthermore, through disobedience, Adam and Eve relinquished having fellowship with God. As a result, humans were immediately catapulted into a state of being "dead in sins and trespasses." Adam and Eve were no longer innocent and alive, but conscience and dead. Being conscience means humans became aware of good and evil. Notice, the "moment their eyes were opened"[178] the Dispensation of Innocence closed and ". . .the Lord God banished [Adam and Eve] from the Garden of Eden. . ."[179]

---

[177] Genesis 2:17 - Easy-to-Read Version (ERV).

[178] Genesis 3:7 - New Living Translation (NLT).

[179] Genesis 3:23 - New Living Translation (NLT).

Working with Unholy, Guilty, and Restless Humans

The Dispensation of Innocence closed in turmoil causing the Dispensation of Conscience to open with all of humanity in an unholy, guilty, and restless state. Due to their instability, "the wickedness of man was great upon the earth."[180] Incapable of diffusing the escalation of turmoil, Humans waxed worst. Humans exuded the evilness of their nature in any manner they could think of. As seen in Genesis 6:5-6:

> *The Lord saw that the wickedness (depravity) of man was great on the earth, and that every imagination or intent of the thoughts of his heart were only evil continually. The Lord [was grieved and He] regretted that He had made [humanity] on the earth.*[181]

Although the wickedness of humans grieved the Master Builder, He still demonstrated His boundless love. Because of His loving kindness He protected His creation. "The Lord's kindness never fails! If He had not been merciful, [God would have destroyed

---

[180] Genesis 6:5 - King James Version (KJV).

[181] Genesis 6:5-6 - Amplified Bible (AMP).

the entire human race]."[182] Instead of destroying humans, the Master Builder consistently unfolded His plans to safeguard His creation. In fact, His plan included a man named Noah. "The name Noah comes from the verbal form of the word *nuach* meaning rest.[183]

Interestingly, the same Master Builder who rested on the seventh day of creation, chose a man whose name means rest to build an Ark that would be the place of rest during the flood. The place of rest required a righteous builder who would follow the Master Builder's blueprint. Also, the builder needed to be someone who would complete the assignment without allowing the sinful nature to alter the plans. Furthermore, the builder needed to be someone who "was without blame in his time. "[184] Being blameless, "Noah found favor in the eyes of the Lord"[185] and the Master Builder gave Noah the blueprints for building an Ark (humongous boat).

Noah followed the blueprints and "built a large boat from cypress wood and waterproofed it with tar, inside and out. Then [he

---

[182] Lamentations 3:22 - Contemporary English Version (CEV).

[183] https://www.ancient-hebrew.org/names/Noah.htm.

[184] Genesis 6:9 - New Life Version (NLV).

[185] Genesis 6:8 - New Life Version (NLV).

constructed] decks and stalls throughout its interior."[186] As the Master Builder continued to reveal His plans, He instructed Noah where to place the door of the [large boat]. "So, Noah did everything exactly as God had commanded him."[187] Noah's faith-filled obedience resulted in his family resting in the Ark as the wrath of God flooded the earth. Once the flood was over, "in the seventh month, on the seventeenth day of the month, the large boat came to rest on Mount Ararat."[188]

After the flood, the new Dispensation of Human Government started with Noah's family. God gave them precise instructions for prospering. However, as Noah and his family began their new journey, there was an uneasiness due to their restless nature. Instead of acknowledging God's commands, the descendants of Noah desired to ease their discomfort by making a name for themselves. Genesis 11:4 puts it like this:

> *The people who lived there began to talk about building a*
> *great city, with a temple-tower reaching to the skies—a*
> *proud, eternal monument to themselves. This will weld us*

---

[186] Genesis 6:14 - New Living Translation (NLT).

[187] Genesis 6:22 - New Living Translation (NLT).

[188] Genesis 8:4 - New Life Version (NLV).

together, they said, "and keep us from scattering all over the world." So, they made great piles of hard burned brick and collected bitumen to use as mortar.[189]

Ignoring the plan and purposes of God, the descendants of Noah were filled with desire, lured by lust, and when desire became the focus and took control, it gave birth to the building of the tower."[190]

Sadly, the descendants of Noah failed the test of obedience. No one took a stand against their rebellion because they all were unholy, guilty, and restless. Each person fulfilled his or her own lustful desires. There is no record of them shouting and praising God for bringing them through the flood. They could barely wait to express their freedom of choice to ignore the plan of God. Step-by-step, they exemplified their true nature of being unthankful, unholy, and untoward God.

The descendants of Noah failed to honor God for allowing them to rest inside the Ark during the flood. In addition, they failed to glorify God for allowing the Ark to rest on Mount Ararat. Furthermore, they failed to trust in the Lord with all their hearts. Leaning to their own understanding, they disobeyed God's

---

[189] Genesis 11:3-4 - Living Bible (TLB).

[190] James 1:14-15 - The Voice (VOICE).

command to scatter and multiply. In their disobedience, Noah's descendants decided to settle in one place. "Then they said, Come, let us build ourselves a city, with a tower that reaches to the heavens. . ."[191] While leaning heavily on their own understanding, they implemented their plans for construction without the Master Builder's authorization.

Just as the Master Builder revealed His blueprint for building the Ark before the flood, He also revealed His blueprint for building the lives of Noah's descendants after the flood. God's precise instructions were scatter and multiply. However, Noah's descendants' finite minds could not comprehend how spreading out in faith and obedience would result in prosperity. Leaning to their own understanding, they said ". . .let's make a name for ourselves, or else we will be scattered over the face of the whole land."[192]

Miserably, leaning to their own understanding, Noah's descendants refused to trust in the Lord with all their hearts. So, they got busy fulfilling their wicked thoughts by setting up an unauthorized construction site. As Noah's descendants hammered away at building their monument of pride, the Master Builder stop

---

[191] Genesis 11:4 - New International Version (NIV).

[192] Genesis 11:4 - Tree of Life Version (TLV).

their devilish construction. Then, "the Lord scattered them abroad from there over the surface of the entire earth; and they stopped building the city."[193] As the restless humans' construction site for building the tower shut down, ". . . the Lord confused the language of the [entire] world. From there the Lord scattered them over the face of the whole earth."[194]

Once again, humans failed to adhere to the Master Builder's blueprints for building wealth. Just to review, in the Dispensation of Innocence, Adam and Eve desired a greater wealth of knowledge. So, they ate from the tree of the knowledge of good and evil. Next, in the Dispensation of Conscience humans desired to build wealth using their finite minds. So much so, they used every evil imagination to build wealth to no avail. Then, in the Dispensation of Human Government, humans desired to make a name for themselves and started a construction site according to their devilish plans.

Due to the rebellion and disobedience of humans the dispensations of Innocence, Conscience, and Human Government closed in judgement. After the Dispensation of Human Government

---

[193] Genesis 11:8 - Amplified Bible (AMP).

[194] Genesis 11:9 - New International Version (NIV).

closed, the Dispensation of Promise opened with Abraham. As seen in prior dispensations, God gave His people unconditional as well as conditional promises. For example, during each dispensation, God gave humans conditional promises to assess their obedience. Contrary to God's plan, in every dispensation, humans failed the test of obedience. Restless and rebellious, humans worked to fulfill "the lust of the flesh, and the lust of the eyes, and the pride of life."[195]

Closing the Dispensation of Promise, God transitioned His people into a new era known as the Dispensation of Law. During the Dispensation of Law, God revealed precise details of His blueprint for staying on the path of ongoing wealth. Notice, He instructed His people through the mouth of Moses saying:

> *Stay on the path that the Lord your God has commanded you to follow. Then you will live long and prosperous lives in the land you are about to enter and occupy.*[196]

The instructions seen in Deuteronomy 5:33 is an extraordinary example of how adhering to God's blueprint will lead to prosperity.

Also, Deuteronomy 6:11 presents a beautiful picture of the benefits of following God's plan. When the Israelites followed the

---

[195] 1 John 2:16 - King James Version (KJV).

[196] Deuteronomy 5:33 - New Living Translation (NLT).

plan of God, He led His people to:

> *houses [that were] richly stocked with goods [they] did not*
> *produce. [They drew] water from cisterns [they] did not dig,*
> *and [they ate] from vineyards and olive trees [they] did not*
> *plant.*[197]

Furthermore, staying on the path that the Lord their God had commanded them to follow caused them to prosper in conquering mightier nations. For instance, they conquered the Hittites, the Girgashites, the Amorites, the Canaanites, the Perizzites, the Hivites, and the Jebusites. As a result, the Israelites experienced prosperity in different dimensions of wealth.

Often, God prospered the Israelites from the perspective of giving them an abundance of rest. For example, Joshua and his brothers needed rest from the brutal attacks of their enemies. So, "the Lord gave them [an abundance of rest from conflict] on every side, in accordance with everything that He had sworn to their fathers, and not one of all their enemies stood before them [in battle]; the Lord handed over all their enemies to them."[198] Keep in mind, Joshua and his brothers practiced adhering to the Master Builder's

---

[197] Deuteronomy 6:11 - New Living Translation (NLT).

[198] Joshua 21:44 - Amplified Bible (AMP).

blueprints for acquiring wealth.

Prospering through faithful obedience is highlighted when, "Joshua called the Reubenites and the Gadites and the half-tribe of Manasseh, and said to them, you have kept all that Moses the servant of the Lord commanded you and have listened to *and* obeyed my voice in everything that I commanded you."[199] In every dispensation the Master Builder reveals His blueprint through a command and/or promise. Then, it is the responsibility of the hearer to act in faithful obedience. As seen throughout the Bible, receiving the Word of God is only part of the requirements for receiving the promise. The other part includes, believing the Word of God and demonstrating faith through careful obedience.

When God's people demonstrate faith through careful obedience, the Master Builder faithfully fulfills His promises. He faithfully reveals His glory, gives insight, and prospers His people in every season of life. However, God warns His people saying:

> *If you start thinking to yourselves, "I did all this. And all by myself. I am rich. It is all mine!"—well, think again. Remember that God, your God, gave you the strength to*

---

[199] Joshua 22:1-2 - Amplified Bible (AMP).

produce all this wealth. . .[200]

Notice, in Deuteronomy 8:17-18, God is counseling Israel to remember Him for being the source of wealth. Even in the Grace Age Dispensation, believers must remember the Master Builder is the One who reveals His glory, gives insight, and prospers His people.

In this Grace Age Dispensation, the Master Builder is revealing His glory and prospering Christians all over the world. Christians are people who partake in the divine nature of God. Prior to being a partaker in the divine nature of God, an individual is unholy, guilty, and restless. However, anyone who follows the plan of salvation by accepting the Master Builder's three-fold invitation, he or she becomes holy, blameless, and restful.

---

[200] Deuteronomy 8:17-18 - The Message (MSG).

Chapter 5

The Master Builder's Three-fold Invitation

The gentle and humble hearted Master Builder is extending a three-part invitation: 1) to find rest in Him, 2) to follow Him, and 3) to build with Him. Unlike seasonal invitations, the Master Builder's invitation is available in every season of life. By God's design, the invitation is available in seasons of sadness or joy, seasons of fear or anger, seasons of surprise or anticipation, and seasons of trust or disgust. Not only is the invitation available during any season of life, but the Master Builder is ever-present to fulfill every aspect of the invitation. Because of His boundless nature, He is everywhere at the same time, and He is willing and able to provide rest, give guidance, and build the lives of His people.

Since the Master Builder is omnipresent, His invitation is also everywhere. Therefore, anyone has access to His invitation from any location. By God's design, people throughout the world can accept the Master Builder's invitation simultaneously and reap the benefits. For example, at high noon, an entrepreneur on the Islands can accept the invitation and get instant assistance for making strategic business decisions. At the same time, another entrepreneur on the other side of the world can except the invitation and receive an immediate answer. Accepting the Master Builder's invitation and reaping the benefits require faith on the behalf of the believer. At all times, faith pleases God.

Believers all over the world are pleasing God through faith-filled obedience. As a result, the boundless Master Builder is taking care of the needs of trillions of Christians simultaneously. While taking care of His people's needs, the Master Builder never gets confused about who needs what. Despite the seasons of life, the omniscient Master Builder knows how to prosper His people both spiritually and naturally. He is not willing for anyone to miss the prosperity that He provides. Therefore, the Master Builder is extending His three-fold invitation to humans from all levels of society.

The invitation from the Master Builder is priceless and is design to give all invitees a wealthy outcome. His three-fold invitation affects every human. Adele Ahlberg Calhoun, declares, "Like tides, His invitation is . . . shaping the contours of [humans'] existence."[201] Despite the fact that humans reject the Master Builder's three-fold invitation, His requests for humans to come unto Him is still shaping their existence. Even though humans

---

[201] Insight gained from - Calhoun, Adele Ahlberg. Invitations from God (Transforming Resources). Page 9.

constantly reject His invitation, the Master Builder faithfully invites humans: to follow Him, to build with Him, and to find rest in Him.

Resting in the Master Builder

Every human that enters the world need to find rest in Christ Jesus. Outside of Christ humans are restless and heavily laden with sin. On one hand, people are thoroughly aware of their restless state. On the other hand, other people are oblivious to the idea of finding rest in Christ. Being ignorant of the fact they need the rest that Jesus offers, people become totally obsessed with acquiring financial wealth. Often, people are successful in building material wealth. But "what good is it for someone to gain the whole world, yet forfeit their soul?"[202]

The Master Builder is not willing for anyone to lose his or her soul. He takes no pleasure in watching humans spend their entire life working to build only temporal wealth. On the contrary, He is willing to allow humans to learn from Him and find rest in Him.[203]

---

[202] Mark 8:36 - New International Version (NIV).

[203] Matthew 11:28-29 - King James Version (KJV).

Although there are various views about who the Lord Jesus is inviting to find rest in Him, one thing is clear – every human needs the rest that Christ Jesus provides. He is the only One who can give rest to all who are weak and heavily laden.

Truly, the Master Builder is the only One who can design an invitation that provides rest from being burden and heavy laden in any situation. Furthermore, He is the only One who can simultaneously meet the needs of all those who accept His invitation. With that thought in mind, marketplace workers can exercise their privilege to benefit from the invitation to rest any time of day or night. For example, anytime a marketplace Christian feels the onset of becoming weary, he or she can cast his or her care over on the Master Builder and continue to rest in Him. Or a non-Christian worker who recognizes the need to find rest in Christ Jesus can accept the invitation to find rest for his or her soul.

Even successful business owners, millionaires, and billionaires can suddenly realize they have a void in their lives that earthly assets cannot fill. At the point of becoming consciously aware of their state of being spiritually poor, business owners, millionaires, and billionaires can find rest in the One who owns everything. The Master Builder is thoroughly aware that people can be successful in the natural realm and still be restless and spiritually poor. In fact, He knows that anyone who endeavors to build wealth using earthly wisdom will eventually become exhausted. Mainly because the Master Builder never intended for humans to carry the weight of temporal wealth without finding balance in Him.

Finding balance in the Master Builder begins with finding rest in Him. When an individual find rest in the Master Builder, he or she becomes receptive to His plan for building wealth. However, the moment an individual who has found rest starts leaning to his or her own understanding he or she can lose balance. When an individual loses balance, he or she can succumb to strategies that are diabolically opposing to the Master Builder's blueprint. As a result, the well-seasoned corporate officer may encounter unexpected outcomes.

Encountering unexpected negative outcomes can be very frustrating! More especially when the expected financial outcome was to be for the sole purpose of increasing employees' pay. Adding to the frustration, management might need to lay off employees to help save the company. However, the reduction in the workforce can lead to overworking of active employees causing an imbalance in their home lives. Next, the overworked employee may eventually take time off from work which could be the catalyst for increased frustration throughout the company.

On any level, when a worker becomes frustrated, he or she can trust and acknowledge God or lean to his or her own understanding. If the marketplace worker leans to his or her own understanding, he or she could compound the situation by making hasty decisions. Or the marketplace worker can trust and acknowledge the Master Builder and reap the benefit of confidently resting in Him. Resting in the Lord and waiting confidently on Him is a sure sign that the believer has a spiritual mindset. In addition, to confidently rest in the Lord is an acknowledgement that God's "thoughts are not [our] thoughts, neither are [our] ways God's ways"[204].

Humans need the superior thoughts and ways of the Master Builder in every facet of life. No one can travel the path of enduring wealth without guidance that comes directly from the mind of God. In every season of life, the Lord's thoughts toward His people are for good. Despite the dark seasons of life, the Master Builder knows how to direct the paths of His people. Since the Master Builder knows all the paths in life, He invites His people to follow Him.

Following the Master Builder

Life is full of swift transitions that can present contrary paths that lead humans away from the plain path of righteousness. Closely following the Master Builder leads to having the victory over the swift transitions of life. In addition, following the Master Builder also guards against the propensity to lean to our own understanding. When humans lean to their own understanding, they follow the dictates of pride and self-righteousness. Instead of following the course of pride and self-righteousness, Christians can closely follow the Master Builder in the plain path of righteousness. In the plain

---

[204] Isaiah 55:8 - King James Version (KJV).

path of righteousness is where Christians learn from the Master Builder as He instructs and council them.

The instructions and the council of the master Builder frees an individual from the deadly grip of being an epicurean. To be clear, an epicurean is a self-willed person who refuses to accept the Master Builder's three-fold invitation. In addition, epicureans let their emotions control them. Also, epicureans have insatiable ambition. The driving force of their greed is pride. As a result, they are citizens of darkness who manifest envy, jealousy, bitterness, and resentment. Sadly, there are self-willed people in the marketplace who are in the deadly grip of being an epicurean.

Self-willed people devote themselves to pursuing sensual pleasures and living a luxurious lifestyle. With that thought in mind, the epicurean lifestyle is an empty way of life that is void of having the peace and prosperity of God. The epicurean lifestyle also leads to disappointment and pessimism. However, even Epicureans have an opportunity to accept the Master Builder's invitation to follow Him. Regardless of the immorality of self-willed individuals, the gentle and humble hearted Master Builder is inviting all self-willed people to follow Him. Accepting the Master Builder's invitation to follow Him in the plain path of righteousness is the only way to forsake being an epicurean.

Once an individual receives deliverance from being an epicurean and faithfully follows the Master Builder, he or she gains clarity concerning the righteousness of God. Other benefits of faithfully following the Master Builder are gaining godly knowledge and godly understanding. In addition, faith-filled followers gain the necessary wisdom to prosper in a godly manner. Not just financial prosperity, but prosperity in every dimension of wealth. While experiencing both spiritual and natural prosperity, Spirit-filled followers should use their wealth to help encourage unbelievers to follow the Master Builder. Encouraging unbelievers to accept the invitation to follow the boundless Master Builder is a demonstration of gratitude and commitment to God.

Demonstrating gratitude and commitment to the Master Builder inspires hope in the workplace. Sadly, people who have not accepted the invitation to follow the Master Builder can experience anguish. Pessimism is the best they can expect from a life lived apart from their Creator. Apart from the Creator, humans are prone to feel despondent because they have a huge void in their lives. Desiring to fill the void, unbelievers seek to fill up on wealth and worldly pleasures.

Ungodly pleasures and temporal wealth will never fill the void the Master Builder left for Himself. Amazingly, when the Master Builder fearfully and wonderfully made humans, He created a space in every human for Himself. When He created Adam and Eve, the Master Builder created them completely whole. God's presence filled their lives, and they had perfect fellowship with God. However, due to their disobedience, Adam and Eve lost fellowship with God. As a result, Adam and Eve experienced the horrific pain of being void of God's presence.

After Adam and Eve lost fellowship with God, their offspring being the entire human race was born with a huge void in their innermost being. Therefore, all humans need the presence of the Holy Spirit – to fill the void that exist in their innermost being. With that thought in mind, owning empires, working for fortune five hundred companies, having a high salary, and/or having high yielding investments cannot fill the void. Neither will large bank accounts, luxury vehicles, or huge homes fill the emptiness that only the Holy Spirit can fill. So, to start the process of having the void filled, an empty individual must receive the precious gift of the Holy Spirit.

When the Spirit of God fills the space that He left for Himself, true believers no longer feel hopeless. In addition, once the Holy Spirit makes His abode in the heart of the believer, He strengthens, energizes, and fortifies the Spirit-filled believer to follow the Master Builder on the path of enduring wealth. Amazingly, as a believer faithfully follows the Master Builder's guidance, he or she remains consciously aware of the fact, "it is God that cause [him or her] to get wealth."[205] In addition, as Spirit-filled

---

[205] Deuteronomy 8:18 - New International Version (NIV).

followers allow the Master Builder to direct their paths, they gain greater insight concerning the Master Builder's blueprints for building wealth.

Building wealth according to the Master Builder's blueprint, Spirit-filled believers experience abundant life. Having abundant life, Christians should be good stewards and use their spiritual and natural wealth for God's glory. As Spirit-filled followers continued to be good stewards, the Master Builder causes them to grow in grace and in the knowledge of God. In addition, Spirit-filled followers gain greater insight into building wealth according to the Master Builder's blueprint.

Building with the Master Builder

The Master Builder is inviting all board members, shareholders, corporate officers, executive officers, and frontline workers to follow His blueprint for building both spiritual and natural wealth. Although His blueprint is precise and infallible, humans still need guidance from the Master Builder during every phase of the building process. Humans cannot follow the Master Builder's principles without the Holy Spirit. Furthermore, humans cannot properly apply God's principles without His wisdom. Without the wisdom of God, the most an unregenerated human can build is temporal wealth using their finite abilities. While temporal wealth can be quite useful in this life, enduring wealth extends far past life as we know it in this world.

Since enduring wealth extends into eternity, humans need divine guidance. With that thought in mind, the Master Builder declares, [He] will teach [His followers] and tell [them] the way to go and how to get there."[206] So, if at any time a believer becomes anxious about building their hopes on things eternal, he or she must continue to trust and acknowledged the infinite Master Builder. He will faithfully direct believers' paths. As the Master Builder directs the steps of believers, they must follow Him in faith.

When true believers please God with faith, He teaches them how to build wealth that glorifies Him. Any time God gets the glory, He keeps on supplying Christians with the necessary building tools to fulfill His plan and purposes. In addition, when Christians build wholeheartedly as unto the Lord, the Master Builder councils them through His Word. For example, in 2 Peter 1:5-9 He advises believers by saying:

> . . . [do not] lose a minute in building on what you have been

---

[206] Psalm 32:8 The Voice Bible (VOICE).

given, complementing your basic faith with good character, spiritual understanding, alert discipline, [enthusiastic] patience, reverent wonder, warm friendliness, and generous love, each dimension fitting into and developing the others. With these qualities active and growing in your lives, no grass will grow under your feet, no day will pass without its reward as you mature in your experience of our Master Jesus. . .[207]

By the power of God, Spirit-filled believers can constantly build spiritual wealth by increasing in good character, spiritual understanding, alert discipline, enthusiastic patience, reverent wonder, warm friendliness, and generous love. Giving greater insight concerning obtaining the gifts of spiritual wealth, the Living Bible explains:

. . . to obtain these gifts, you need more than faith; you must also work hard to be good, and even that is not enough. For then you must learn to know God better and discover what he wants you to do.[208]

The only way to learn the intricate details of what God wants us to

---

[207] 2 Peter 1:5-9 - The Message (MSG).

[208] 2 Peter 1:5 - Living Bible (TLB).

do is to yoke up with the Master Builder and learn from Him. He thoroughly understands every aspect of the blueprint for building both spiritual and natural wealth. By God's design, the omniscient Master Builder is willing to go into partnership with finite humans and reveal His infallible building plan.

Being in partnership with the boundless Master Builder has endless benefits. The benefits include freedom from the grip of spiritual poverty and having restored fellowship with God. Also, being in partnership with the Master Builder gives Christians the authority to build wealth both spiritually and naturally for God's glory. While prospering in the natural realm is important, the most enduring prosperity is spiritual wealth.

Chapter 6

Spiritual Wealth

God eternally purposed for humans to be spiritually wealthy in this present world. He is seen unveiling His plan in Genesis 2:7:

> *The Lord God formed the man from the soil of the ground and breathed into his nostrils the breath of life, and the man became a living being.*[209]

The very moment the man "Adam" became a living being, he was everything God purposed for him to be. He was in perfect union with God and spiritually wealthy.

God placed the spiritually wealthy man in the Garden of Eden to dress it and to keep it. But notice in Genesis 2:16-17:

> *the Lord God commanded the man, saying, of every tree of the garden thou mayest freely eat: But of the tree of the knowledge of good and evil, thou shalt not eat of it: for in the day that thou eatest thereof thou shalt surely die.*[210]

---

[209] Genesis 2:7 - New English Translation (NET).

[210] Genesis 2:16-17 - King James Version (KJV).

Notice, the Edenic Covenant is a conditional covenant. The stipulations that God set forth in the covenant includes seven main parts:

Stipulation #1	Humans are commanded to reproduce spiritually wealthy descendants who would reflect the image of God in the manner they were originally created.	Genesis 1:28a
Stipulation #2	Humans are given authority over the earth.	Genesis 1:28b
Stipulation #3	Humans are given authority over the animal kingdom.	Genesis 1:28c
Stipulation #4	Humans are given permission to eat vegetation.	Genesis 1:29-30
Stipulation #5	Humans are given the responsibility to dress and keep the Garden of Eden.	Genesis 2:15
Stipulation #6	Humans are warned not to eat from the Tree of the Knowledge of Good and Evil.	Genesis 2:17a
Stipulation #7	The punishment for violating the covenant is death; both spiritually and physically.	Genesis 2:17b

As seen in Genesis 2:17b, the consequence for violating the covenant is death.

Sadly, Adam and Eve failed the test of obedience and broke the Edenic Covenant. Giving greater insight Apostle Paul explains:

This, then, is what happened. Sin made its entry into the world through one man, and through sin, death. The entail of sin and death passed on to the whole human race, and no one could break it for no one was himself free from sin. Sin, you see, was in the world long before the Law, though I suppose, technically speaking, it was not "sin" where there was no law to define it. Nevertheless death, the complement of sin, held sway over mankind from Adam to Moses, even over those whose sin was quite unlike Adam's. . .[211]

The Bible makes it plain how the grip of spiritual poverty became evident the moment Adam and Eve broke the Edenic Covenant.

Caught in the grip of spiritual deprivation, Adam and Eve were incapable of reproducing spiritually wealthy descendants. Therefore, all their descendants are spiritually traumatized, exhausted, and heavily laden. In fact, at the time of conception, all humans are intoxicated and immobilized by the filthy stench of being spiritually dead in trespasses and sins. Being spiritually dead means an individual is alienated from having fellowship with God. Nevertheless, God desires to restore humans to their intended purpose through reconciliation and sanctification.

---

[211] Romans 5:12-14 - J.B. Phillips New Testament (PHILLIPS).

The Master Builder's Blueprint for Building Enduring Wealth

The Bible reveals, it is through the atoning work of Christ, humans can call on the name of the Lord and be reconciled with God. The substitutional sacrifice of Christ opened the door for humans to experience forgiveness and receive the Holy Spirit. The presence of the Holy Spirit in the life of the believer is evidence that he or she is experiencing the authentic power of reconciliation. Also, being sealed with the promise of the Holy Spirit means an individual's spiritual wealth has been restored.

Various aspects of spiritual wealth include godly wisdom, godly knowledge, and godly understanding. Also, the Fruit of the Spirit, the revelation of God, and the treasure of the Gospel are facets of spiritual wealth. Still further, growing in grace and growing in the knowledge of Jesus Christ are other ways Christians increase in spiritual wealth. Increasing in spiritual wealth empowers Christians to "lay up for [themselves] treasures in heaven."[212]

Having the power to lay up treasures in heaven begins with the believer receiving the Holy Spirit. Through and by the Holy Spirit, Christians gain a restored fellowship with God. Having fellowship with God gives Christians direct access to commune with God in prayer. With assistance from the Holy Spirit, Christians can build themselves upon their most holy faith. As a result, Christians ". . . rise like an edifice higher and higher."[213] Unlike the prophets of old, Christians have the privilege to pray in the Holy Spirit.

Although the Spirit of God moved upon the prophets of old, they did not have the indwelling power of the Holy Spirit. Therefore, the prophets of old could not pray in the new dimension of prayer that Christians are authorized to pray in. Even the disciples who walk with Jesus did not pray in the Holy Spirit before receiving power from on high. Notice, the Master Builder who taught Peter, James, and John how to pray also instructed them to wait in the Upper Room for the infilling of the Holy Spirit. At the very moment Peter, James, and John received God's power, they were

---

[212] Matthew 6:20 - New International Version (NIV).

[213] Jude 20 - Amplified Bible (AMP).

immediately authorized to pray in the Holy Spirit.

Miraculously, Peter, James, and John ". . . who months before had been impulsive, competitive, bickering, cowering, and deserting their Lord - were transformed by the Holy Spirit on the inside."[214] Through and by the indwelling power of the Holy Spirit, they prayed in a new dimension of prayer. Not just Peter, James, and John, but on the Day of Pentecost in the Upper Room there were one hundred and seventeen other souls who received the Holy Spirit and prayed in a new dimension. According to God's eternal plan, on that same day approximately three thousand other souls received the Holy Spirit and received power to pray in a new dimension. The power to pray in a new dimension is another aspect of gaining spiritual wealth.

Another extraordinary example of someone gaining the power to pray in the Holy Spirit is the Apostle Paul. Also known as Saul of Tarsus, Paul was guilty of fighting against the disciples of Christ. He was oblivious to the fact that he was opposing spiritually wealthy believers who had learned how to pray in a new dimension. While Saul of Tarsus was in the grip of spiritual poverty, he persecuted the Church. Like every human that enters the world spiritually poor, Paul needed deliverance from being in

---

[214] Kim Avery (p. 45).

spiritual poverty.

Although Paul was "of the people of Israel, of the tribe of Benjamin, and a Hebrew of Hebrews. . ."[215] – he still needed the power of the Holy Spirit. Notice what he cries out as he reflects on his sinful nature, "[I have] tried everything, and nothing helps. I am at the end of my rope. Is there no one who can do anything for me?"[216] Paul was describing the agony of being born spiritually dead. But something wonderful happened once he had an encounter with the Master Builder. By God's design, Paul received eternal life in Christ Jesus.

The very moment Paul received eternal life in Christ Jesus, he could pray in a new dimension. While praying in a new dimension of prayer, Paul increased in godly wisdom, godly knowledge, and godly understanding. He also manifested the Fruit of the Spirit. Like Paul, marketplace Christians can exercise their privilege to pray in the Holy Spirit. Also, with assistance from the Holy Spirit, believers can demonstrate the Fruit of the Spirit. As Christians experience and show an abundance of "love, joy, peace, forbearance, kindness, goodness, faithfulness, gentleness and self-

---

[215] Philippians 3:5- New International Version (NIV).

[216] Romans 7:24 - The Message (MSG).

control,"[217] they grow in grace.

While growing in grace and prayerfully moving through the workday, Christian workers glorify God in every sphere of the marketplace. As a tent maker, Paul was familiar with glorifying God in the marketplace. Glorifying God in the workplace can be the catalyst for Christians connecting with others of like faith. For example, Paul "met a Jew named Aquila, a native of Pontus, who had recently come from Italy with his wife Priscilla, because Claudius had ordered all Jews to leave Rome. Nevertheless, the providential workings of God were evident in the lives of Aquila and Priscilla.

By God's design, Aquila and Priscilla divinely connected with Paul. As seen in Acts 18:1-3:

> *. . . Paul left Athens and went to Corinth. There he met a Jew named Aquila, a native of Pontus, who had recently come from Italy with his wife Priscilla, because Claudius had ordered all Jews to leave Rome. Paul went to see them, and because he was a tentmaker as they were, he stayed and* [collaborated] *with them.*[218]

---

[217] Galatians 5:22-23 - New International Version (NIV).

[218] Acts 18:1-3 - New International Version (NIV).

No doubt, as Paul worked with Aquila and Priscilla, he practiced praying in the workplace. In addition to praying in the workplace, Paul spent personal time communing with God in prayer. Paul built himself "up in [his] most holy faith [as he prayed] in the Holy Spirit."[219] As a result, Paul grew in grace as well as in the knowledge of Jesus Christ. In other words, the more Paul prayed in the Holy Spirit, the more he increased in spiritual wealth. Paul was so spiritually wealthy that he was no longer persecuting the people of God but praying for them.

Paul prayed for other believers to increase spiritually. For instance, in Philippians 1:9, Paul prayed, "I pray that your love will keep on growing more and more, together with true knowledge and perfect judgment."[220] As seen in Paul's prayer, growing in love, true knowledge, and perfect judgement are ways Christians increase in spiritual wealth. Also, having the eyes of our heart enlightened is another example of increasing spiritually. During one of Paul's prayers, he expressed his desire for believers' ". . .minds [to be] opened to see [God's] light, so that [believers] will know what is the hope to which [God called believers], how rich are the wonderful

---

[219] Jude 1:20 - New International Version (NIV).

[220] Philippians 1:9 - Good News Translation (GNT).

130

blessings [God] promises His people."[221]

Paul's prayers show his love for God as well as other people. Further observation of Paul's prayers reveals the source of Christians' hope. For example, Paul prayed, "May God, the source of hope, fill you with all joy and peace by means of your faith in him, so that your hope will continue to grow by the power of the Holy Spirit."[222] Paul's prayer reveals three great truths: 1) God is the source of our hope, 2) believers are filled with joy and peace by means of their faith in God; and 3) believers increase in spiritual wealth by the Holy Spirit. By God's design, this same Paul encourages believers to pray in the Spirit.[223]

Praying in the Holy Spirit is a dimension of prayer where God releases a wealth of knowledge and understanding. Also, while praying in the Holy Spirit believers increase in godly wisdom. Having godly wisdom is key to winning souls for Christ. Using godly wisdom, Christians can help deliver people who are in the grip of spiritual poverty. For example, Christians can use the wisdom of God to properly discern the opportune time to share the Gospel of

---

[221] Ephesians 1:18 - Good News Translation (GNT).

[222] Romans 15:13 - Good News Translation (GNT).

[223] Ephesians 6:18 – Darby Translation (DARBY).

Jesus Christ. Christians can also use godly wisdom to encourage other marketplace Christians.

In the marketplace, Christians are known for exercising godly wisdom to shift the atmosphere in staff meetings, shareholders' meetings, and board meetings. In various business meetings, Christians use godly wisdom to secure business contracts. Coupled with faith in God, Christians use godly wisdom to make prudent business decisions that change the trajectory of the entire corporation. Even frontline Christian workers use the wisdom of God as they supply outstanding customer service. When Christian workers on any level, use godly wisdom in the workplace, God reveals His glory, gives insight, and prospers His people.

While God is at work revealing His glory, giving insight, and prospering His people, the Holy Spirit illuminates Christians. As the Holy Spirit illuminates Christians, the Master Builder councils them saying:

> *You are like that illuminating light. Let your light shine everywhere you go, that you may illumine creation, so* [people] *everywhere may see your good actions, may see creation at its fullest, may see your devotion to Me, and may*

turn and praise your Father in heaven because of it.[224]

As unbelievers turn and praise God, Christians' adoration for the Lord increases.

A Wealth of Adoration

Christians who have grown in grace and in the knowledge of the Lord Jesus Christ have a wealth of adoration for God. A wealth of adoration for God inspires believers to acknowledge the Lord in all their ways. In addition, the adoration that Christians have for God inspires them to trust the lord wholeheartedly despite the happenings of the marketplace. Christians who reverence God and keep His commandments have the spiritual fortitude to keep their minds stayed on the Master Builder throughout the workday. Because of their love and adoration for God, Christians guard against the contamination of Secular Humanism.

As Secular Humanism increases, there is a blatant deterioration of reverence for God. In every corner of the marketplace, Secular Humanism exalts self to be its own god. Contrary to the Word of God, secular humanism opposes the existence of the Eternal God. Leaning to their own understanding,

---

[224] Matthew 5:16 - The Voice (VOICE).

secular humanists have formed their own concepts concerning morality. For example, Phil Zuckerman Ph.D. informs:

> *Secular Humanism frames morality as not causing unnecessary pain, harm, or suffering to humans and other animals; easing or relieving the pain or sufferings of humans and other animals, comforting those who are vulnerable or weak; working to increase health, happiness, and well-being in our families, communities, and society at large; fighting for fairness and justice; being empathetic and compassionate; being honest, conscientious, and caring; treating people the way in which we ourselves would want to be treated.*[225]

On the surface, Secular Humanism presents ideas that coincide with Biblical principles. For example, the Bible emphatically states, "do for others what you want them to do for you. This is the teaching of the laws of Moses [concisely]."[226] On that note, Christians are known for performing the same charitable deeds that secular humanists perform. However, Christians' charitable deeds show their love for God and His people. Unlike

---

[225] https://www.psychologytoday.com/us/blog/the-secular-life/202002/what-is-secular-humanism

[226] Matthew 7:12 - Living Bible (TLB).

Christians, secular humanists perform all their charitable deeds without having a love and adoration for God.

Sadly, the mentality of the secular humanist is set on self-reliance, self-exaltation, and self-righteousness. Contrary to God's blueprint, the secular humanist believes all accomplishments in life comes from the abilities of finite humans. In addition, from the secular humanist's perspective, it does not make sense to trust or acknowledge God. Zuckerman explains:

> *Secular Humanism begins with denial or doubt concerning the existence of anything supernatural - including God - but then goes well beyond that secular stance by positively affirming and valuing the potential of human beings to be kind, enact justice, solve problems, and make the world a better, safer, greener, and more humane place.*[227]

Despite the philosophies of secular humanism, Christian workers reverence and glorify the Master Builder in every sphere of the marketplace. As wise sons and daughters of God, Christian frontline workers are exuding a wealth of adoration for God in staff meetings. As a result, God is prospering His people and allowing them to exude the Fruit of the Spirit as they interact in meetings.

---

[227] https://www.psychologytoday.com/us/blog/the-secular-life/202002/what-is-secular-humanism.

Through awe-filled worship, Christian frontline workers are also spreading the fragrance of God's peace in every business transaction.

In awe of God, Christian executive officers show their reverence for God in stockholders' meetings and board meetings. Christian executive officers also demonstrate their reverence for God as they interact with competing businesses. Not just seasoned workers and executives reverence God, but even newly hired Christian workers show a reverence during the new hire process. As Christian workers reverence God in all they do, He allows them to gain greater knowledge about the thoughts and ways of God.

A Wealth of Godly Knowledge

Gaining a wealth of godly knowledge should be the aspiration of every human. On the contrary, people from all levels of society invest vast amounts of money and energy to achieve a wealth of natural knowledge. Researchers as well as Scientists are constantly investing time investigating the boundaries of human's understanding in effort to gain greater knowledge and to find medical breakthroughs. Learning institutions around the world supply countless classes for people of all ages who are hoping to become more educated. Apart from learning institutions, children, young adults, and seniors explore the internet to increase their knowledge.

Knowledge is a powerful tool, both spiritually and naturally. From a natural perspective, the possession of knowledge is an extraordinary gift. Humans use knowledge to pursue great ambitions. Even during challenging times, if an individual has knowledge, he or she can discover the necessary resources to overcome obstacles. In addition, individuals who have natural knowledge have an awareness of how to move forward when others are confused. Amazingly, when knowledge is properly integrated and used to make the right business decisions in the marketplace, it grows to be wisdom.

Making prudent business decisions can produce great riches. Producing vast amounts of riches sounds like the perfect time to boast. However, the Master Builder informs in Jeremiah 9:23-24:

> *Let not the wise man bask in his wisdom, nor the mighty man in his might, nor the rich man in his riches. Let them boast in this alone: That they truly know me and understand that I am the Lord of justice and of righteousness whose love is steadfast. . .*[228]

The knowledge of God is more valuable than great riches. It supersedes common sense and book knowledge. The knowledge of

---

[228] Jeremiah 9:23-24 - Living Bible (TLB).

God gives insight concerning His character and nature. In addition, the knowledge of God will align one's speech, thoughts, and actions with the Master Builder's blueprint.

Saul of Tarsus is a splendid example of how an educated person still needs to have his or her speech, thoughts, and actions aligned with God's blueprint. History reveals, at an early age, Saul's mother and father trained him in fundamental principles according to the law of Moses. When Saul became a teenager, he started learning the marketplace skill of tent making. While still in his teens, Saul received an education in Jewish Orthodoxy at the College of Rabbis. Interestingly, Rabbi Gamaliel who was a learned Pharisee, a doctor of the law, and one of the greatest teachers of his day trained Saul.

Saul was very educated, he had a fervent zeal for God, and he gained great leadership status in Judaism. Despite having profound knowledge concerning the law, Saul still needed to gain insight about God being the Lord of justice and of righteousness. In addition, Saul needed to have his speech, thoughts, and actions properly aligned with Gods blueprint. Of course, after Saul experienced being born of the water and of the Spirit, he stood strong and prevailed against the tactics of the adversary.

While prevailing against the tactics of the adversary, Paul built himself upon his most holy faith by praying in the Holy Spirit. Paul worshipped and praised God for delivering him from the grip of spiritual poverty. As a result, God prospered Paul and gave him an abundance of revelations, wisdom, knowledge, and understanding. As seen in the Bible, Paul increased in spiritual wealth. For God's glory, he used his spiritual wealth to teach other believers how to prosper spiritually.

Paul made it clear, the only way to increase spiritually is to lay earthly possessions at the feet of the Lord Jesus Christ. As seen in Philippians 3:8-9, Paul:

> . . . *counted everything as loss compared to the priceless privilege and supreme advantage of knowing Christ Jesus [our] Lord [and of growing more deeply and thoroughly acquainted with Him—a joy unequaled]. For [Jesus Christ's] sake [Paul] lost everything, and [he considered] it all garbage, so that [he] may gain Christ, and may be found in Him [believing and relying on Him], not having any righteousness of [his] own derived from [his obedience to] the Law and its rituals, but [possessing] that [genuine righteousness] which comes through faith in Christ, the righteousness which comes from God on the basis of faith.*[229]

Learning from Apostle Paul's example, when Christian workers' speech, thoughts, and actions are in alignment with the will

---

[229] Philippians 3:8 & 9 - Amplified Bible (AMP).

of God, they adhere to God's blueprint. In addition, Christians who truly know God and understand that He is the Lord of justice and of righteousness whose love is steadfast, they will do exploits. Daniels 11:32 declares, ". . . the people who know their God will stand strong and prevail."[230] Although Daniels 11:32 was giving reference to the Maccabees who led a heroic revolt against Antiochus, the truth of the verse is profitable for instructions in righteousness.

Christians like Peter, James, John, Paul, and Silas knew their God and were able to effectively resist the forces of darkness. Understanding the importance of knowing God, Apostle Peter encourages Christians to "grow in the grace and knowledge of our Lord and Savior Jesus Christ."[231] Growing in the knowledge of our Lord and Savior Jesus Christ comes from having an intimate relationship with Him. In addition, increasing in the knowledge of Jesus Christ involves spiritual discipline such as praying, fasting, and studying the Bible.

Having greater insight concerning the Lord, Christians can glorify God in every season of life. For example, a faith-filled business owner will praise and glorify God even when they

---

[230] Daniel 11:32 - Tree of Life Version (TLV).

[231] 2 Peter 3:18 - New International Version (NIV). New International Version (NIV).

experience a decrease in sales. Despite having a need in the natural realm, the Christian owner walks by faith glorifying God every step of the way. Why? Because the Spirit-filled business owner is thoroughly persuaded that "God will meet all [his or her] needs according to the riches of [God's] glory in Christ Jesus."[232] The Christian owner also knows God is at work in his or her life giving him or her an opportunity to glorify God by using godly wisdom.

A Wealth of Godly Wisdom

Godly "wisdom is the principal thing"[233] for building both natural and spiritual wealth. Since godly wisdom is essential for building enduring wealth, the Master Builder gives precise instructions for getting wisdom. To start the process of getting godly wisdom, an individual must reverence the One who is infinite in wisdom. Notice, Proverbs 9:10 states, "the fear of the Lord is the beginning of wisdom. . ."[234] When an individual fears the Lord, he or she starts the journey of getting godly wisdom. As believers receive and use godly wisdom, God reveals His glory.

---

[232] Philippians 4:19 - New International Version (NIV).

[233] Proverbs 4:7 - King James Version (KJV).

[234] Proverbs 9:10a - King James Version (KJV).

Wonderful things happen in every season of life as God reveals His glory. In addition to gaining wisdom, believers gain greater knowledge concerning God's principles. Interestingly, having knowledge of God's principles is good. But having the necessary wisdom to apply the principle is the catalyst for experiencing prosperity. Although knowledge alone is powerful, the believer must use godly wisdom to skillfully apply the Master Builder's principles. When believers properly apply the Master Builder's wealth-building principles they prosper both spiritually and naturally.

As believers prosper on the path of enduring wealth, they soon realize the link between using godly wisdom and getting wealth. As a result, believers develop a desire for more of God's wisdom. In addition to gaining wealth, there are other reasons why believers want a constant flow of God's wisdom. For example, godly wisdom "is first pure, then peaceable, gentle, and easy to be intreated, full of mercy and good fruits, without partiality, and without hypocrisy."[235] By God's design, godly wisdom is full of spiritual wealth.

Using the wisdom of God, Christians can shift the atmosphere of the workplace. For God's glory, in every sphere of the marketplace, Christians can use the peaceable aspect of wisdom

---

[235] James 3:17 - King James Version (KJV).

to create a positive workplace culture. Of course, coupled with peace, other aspects such as gentleness, honesty, and mercy will also help to maintain a positive workplace culture. In addition to creating and supporting a peaceful work environment, corporate and executive officers can use godly wisdom to make strategic, operational, and/or financial decisions. As a result, every worker in the corporation will reap the benefit.

In addition to using godly wisdom to make prudent business decisions, Christian managers can use godly wisdom to promote compassion. Since there are times when employees may feel overworked and underpaid, managers can use godly wisdom to express empathy. One situation that comes to mind is a frontline worker who is on the verge of quitting because she feels unappreciated. She had her resignation letter prepared to quit at the end of the day. However, the department manager properly discerned the situation, used godly wisdom, and encouraged the frontline worker. Once the frontline worker heard the kind words that came from the Christian manager, she reframed from giving her letter of resignation.

Seven months later, the frontline worker who was on the verge of quitting replaced the manager who encouraged her. But the story gets better, the original manager became vice president of the company. Careful observation of the scenario reveals how God rewards believers who are committed to using godly wisdom. God did not forget the manager's labor of love. In fact, He rewarded the

Christian manager for using godly wisdom to speak kind words in due season.

In addition to speaking kind words in due season, Christian workers can use godly wisdom to refrain from speaking during inappropriate times. Godly wisdom dictates to the heart of the believer when to speak and when to keep silent. The wisdom of God also teaches believers how to practice honoring God with their lives through faith-filled obedience. Adhering to God's plans, Christian workers "grow in spiritual strength and become better acquainted with our Lord and Savior Jesus Christ."[236] As a result, Christians gain greater insight concerning the wisdom of God revealed in Christ Jesus.

God's Wisdom Revealed in Christ Jesus

Without the wisdom of God, humans use earthly wisdom. "Such wisdom does not come down from heaven but is earthly, unspiritual, and demonic."[237] Earthly wisdom cannot manifest sanctification, redemption, godly righteousness, or eternal life. So, earthly wisdom offers no hope of receiving eternal salvation.

---

[236] 2 Peter 3:18 - Living Bible (TLB).

[237] James 3:15 - New International Version (NIV).

Furthermore, humans cannot use earthly wisdom to escape spiritual poverty. The only way humans escape spiritual deprivation is through the wisdom of God revealed in Christ.

The wisdom of God revealed in Christ Jesus is the only solution for securing eternal salvation. In Christ alone, believers obtain sanctification, redemption, righteousness, and eternal life. Christ Jesus paid the ultimate price to release humans from the grip of spiritual poverty. To be clear, Christ Jesus purchased our redemption with something greater than silver or gold. He redeemed all Spirit-filled believers with His precious blood. Based on the infinite wisdom of God, through the blood of Christ Jesus believers are free from the grip of spiritual poverty.

Since sanctification, redemption, righteousness, and eternal life is in Christ alone, no one can say his or her wisdom contributed to his or her freedom. In Christ alone, believers are recipients of God's wisdom. In Christ alone, believers are the righteousness of God. 2 Corinthians 5:21 explains how God:

> . . . *made Christ who knew no sin to judicially be sin on our behalf, so that in Him [believers] would become the righteousness of God. . .*[238]

---

[238] 2 Corinthians 5:21 - Amplified Bible (AMP).

Glory be to God, all Spirit-filled believers have fellowship with our heavenly Father - in Christ alone.

All because of the boundless wisdom and love of God, humans who died in the first Adam is alive in the second Adam. In addition, the second Adam recovered the spiritual wealth lost through the disobedience of the first Adam. Through the finished work of Christ believers are heirs to the promises of God. Being heirs to the promises of God, believers can freely use God's treasures.

The treasure that God has given to all believers includes a new heart, the love of God, the glorious gospel, the Spirit of the Lord, and the abiding presence of the boundless Master Builder. The new heart has a wealth of God's love by the Spirit of the Lord. In addition, through and by the love and grace of God, the riches of the glorious gospel fill the hearts of believers. Still further, the Master Builder faithfully works in the hearts of believers empowering them to increase in spiritual balance and spiritual discipline for His glory.

Chapter 7
Spiritual Discipline and Balance

Believers need spiritual discipline and balance to build enduring wealth. Keep in mind, spiritual discipline and balance are not one-time events or achievements, they are the wealth building blend of a God-fearing lifestyle. By God's design, spiritual discipline is the work out phase for building a wealth of spiritual balance. Just as physical exercises strengthen the body to meet the challenges of life, the spiritual exercises of prayer and fasting strengthen our confidence in the Master Builder. Coupled with prayer and fasting, reading the Bible cultivates our faith. Through the power of faith, we can stay balanced by focusing on the One who is able to keep us from falling.

The Master Builder is the One who keeps Christians from falling back to the beggarly elements of the world. He supplies spiritual stability for Christians who trust Him wholeheartedly. Believers need to have stability when they see ungodly people prospering more than the righteous. With that thought in mind, Christians can identify with the Psalmist who wrote, "my feet came close to stumbling, my steps had almost slipped. For I was envious of the arrogant as I saw the prosperity of the wicked."[239] However, even at the point of almost slipping, the Lord will uphold anyone that cries out like Peter and say "Lord, save me!"[240]

Any time Christian workers cry out to the Lord, He will supply spiritual balance. Having spiritual balance believers can stand strong in the Lord and obey the command seen in Titus 2:12:

> . . . *reject ungodliness and worldly (immoral) desires, and to live sensible, upright, and godly* – [living] *with a purpose that reflect spiritual maturity in this present age* . . .[241]

Having spiritual balance, marketplace Christians can also resist the temptations of the marketplace.

By God's design, spiritual discipline, and balance do not involve laws that work against Christian workers, but laws that work for their good in every dimension of wealth. In fact, through spiritual discipline and balance Christians achieve complete freedom and victory through the Boundless Master Builder. Having spiritual balance, with God's help, believers can successfully maneuver

---

[239] Psalm 73:2 & 3 - Amplified Bible (AMP).

[240] Matthew 14:30 - Amplified Bible (AMP).

[241] Titus 2:12 - Amplified Bible (AMP).

through the unpleasant seasons of life.

Although Christians will encounter situations designed to throw them off balance, they can remain:

> *steadfast, immovable, always abounding in the work of the Lord - always being superior, excelling, doing more than enough in the service of the Lord, knowing and being continually aware that [their] labor in the Lord is not futile - it is never wasted or to no purpose.*[242]

The Master Builder has a purpose for allowing Christian workers to encounter situations that could cause an imbalance. He wants Christians to know Him as being the anchor of their soul. He also wants believers to know He gives spiritual stability in the tempestuous seasons of life.

Situations that could cause an imbalance are opportunities for faith-filled followers to trust in the Lord with all their heart. Challenging times are opportunities for Christians to practice spiritual discipline and balance. Just like Paul and Silas glorified God in challenging situations, Christians can also use spiritual discipline and balance to glorify God during adversities. Notice, Paul, and Silas exuded spiritual discipline and balance as they preached and serve

---

[242] 1 Corinthians 15:58 - Amplified Bible, Classic Edition (AMPC).

Jesus Christ everywhere they ministered. Even when in prison, Paul and Silas demonstrated spiritual discipline and balance.[243]

Despite harsh conditions, Paul and Silas prayed and sang praises to God. Both were determined to stay on the path of enduring wealth. The two ambassadors of the Lord were on a divine assignment giving them an opportunity to follow the Master Builder's blueprint. Yes, the part that says, "Trust in the Lord with all your heart and lean not on your own understanding; in all your ways submit to him, and he will make your paths straight."[244] Even when the paths of Christians intercept with the crooked and treacherous paths of the ungodly, the Master Builder will continue to make the paths of the godly straight. The Lord kept His promise and delivered Paul and Silas.

After his prison experience, the Apostle Paul encouraged Christians to pray without ceasing. Notice, "the Greek word translated to *without ceasing* is αδιαλειπτως (adialeíptōs), which means constantly or without intermission."[245] With that thought in

---

[243] Acts 16:16-36 - Living Bible (TLB).

[244] proverbs 3:5-6 - New International Version (NIV).

[245] https://www.biblestudytools.com/bible-study/topical-studies/can-we-really-pray-without-ceasing.html.

mind, Paul was encouraging the people of God to constantly pray about everything. Paul emphasized the importance of making prayer a priority. Why? Because prayer is a spiritual discipline that increases spiritual balance. Since spiritual balance is a requirement for staying on the path of enduring wealth, Christians must practice the spiritual discipline of prayer.

Long before Paul and Silas were born, Daniel exemplified spiritual discipline and balance. Using his wealth of spiritual discipline and balance, Daniel remained confident. However, Daniel was not confident because he was skillful in all wisdom and quick to understand. He was not confident because of his intelligence and discernment. Daniel's confidence was in the Lord, and he acknowledged the Lord in all his ways. So much so,

> *Daniel* [was determined] *in his heart that he would not defile himself with the portion of the king's meat, nor with the wine which he drank: therefore, he requested of the prince of the eunuchs that he might not defile himself. Now God had brought Daniel into favor and tender love with the prince of the eunuchs.*[246]

---

[246] Daniel 1:8 - King James Version (KJV).

Daniel loved the communion he had with the King of kings. Speaking of communion with God, Daniel's prayer life is an extraordinary demonstration of spiritual discipline. For instance, "Daniel always prayed to God. . . Three times every day, he bowed down on his knees to pray and praise God. . . "[247] Through the spiritual discipline of prayer, Daniel maintained his spiritual balance. Using spiritual discipline and balance, Daniel increased in spiritual wealth. He refused to exchange his spiritual wealth for the temporal wealth of Babylon.

Even after King Darius implemented a law against praying, Daniel remained confident in God and continued to pray three times every day. Daniel practiced the discipline of prayer because he knew all his help came from the Lord. Daniel also understood prayer is a perfect gift from God. Out of all the other gifts Daniel possessed, he used prayer as His primary method for reaching God. During success and adversities, Daniel skillfully used the gift of prayer as he exuded faith and trust in God.

No doubt, Daniel's prayer life was a time of refreshment on the path of enduring wealth. As Daniel bowed before the Lord, he received greater insight on using his gifts for God's glory. But notice,

[247] Daniel 6:10-28 - Easy-to-Read Version (ERV).

despite Daniel's dedication to communing with God, he still met challenging times. Daniel had an excellent spirit, and he had favor with God and man, but according to the Master Builder's blueprint, Daniel still had to go through challenging times. In fact, everyone who practice living a godly life in Christ Jesus will encounter challenging times.[248]

Without exception, all Christians will go through unpleasant seasons. In every sphere of the marketplace Christians encounter tough times. Even entry level Christians encounter inconvenient situations. Nevertheless, God is faithfully ordering the paths of marketplace Christians. The boundless Master Builder is also strengthening Christian workers on every level as they exude bold confidence in Him. In addition, the Lord is allowing Christian workers to grow in grace as they encounter persecution in the marketplace.

During times of persecution, the boundless Master Builder has always delivered those who walk upright before Him. He faithfully takes care of believers who reverence Him and keep His commandments. However, reverencing God and keeping His commandments does not exempt Christians from experiencing

---

[248] 2 Timothy 3:12 – Holman Christian Standard Bible (HCSB).

persecution in the workplace. By God's design, persecution presents an opportunity for Christians to exercise faith in God. In fact, Christians can use the gift of prayer to commune with God and receive greater insight during trouble. Just like God delivered Daniel, He will deliver all those who trust in the Lord.

Although Daniel encountered great persecution, the Lord faithfully directed Daniel's paths. But the narrative of how God directed Daniel's paths - is quite surprising. More especially since God ordered Daniel's paths to the center stage of the lions' den. God strategically led Daniel to a stage that was divinely set by the boundless Master Builder. The very stage where He would show Himself strong on Daniel's behalf. Even in the den of lions, God allowed Daniel to prosper and have good success. Remember, the same God who prospered Daniel in the den of lions is the same God who has eternally purpose to prosper Christians in the marketplace.

Christians can prosper in the workplace without compromising godly principles. If Christian workers continue to live godly in every aspect of life, God will prosper them both spiritually and naturally. Learning from Daniel's example, Christians must purpose in their heart not to defile themselves by accepting ungodly portions of wealth. Acceptance of ungodly portions of wealth equates to willfully leaving the path of enduring wealth. In addition, leaning to one's own finite understanding is a refusal to trust the Lord. But the good news is Christians who reverence God and keep His commandments gain a greater adoration for the Master Builder.

Sadly, in this Grace Age Dispensation, there is a blatant deterioration of reverence for God as Secular Humanism increases. In every corner of the marketplace, Secular Humanism exalts self to be its own god. Secular Humanism opposes the existence of the Eternal God. Leaning to their own understanding, secular humanists have formed their own concepts concerning morality. As stated by Phil Zuckerman:

> *Secular Humanism frames morality as not causing unnecessary pain, harm, or suffering to humans and other animals; . . . fighting for fairness and justice; being empathetic and compassionate; being honest, conscientious, and caring . . .*[249]

Of course, easing or relieving the pain or suffering of humans and comforting those who are vulnerable are charitable deeds. However, the secular humanist performs charitable deeds without trusting and acknowledging God. In addition, the secular

---

[249] https://www.psychologytoday.com/us/blog/the-secular-life/202002/what-is-secular-humanism.

humanist believes all accomplishments in life happen through the power and might of finite beings. Nevertheless, Christians perform the same charitable deeds to glorify God. In fact, believers practice "[seeking] first the kingdom of God and His righteousness."[250]

All humans should follow the command to seek God first. However, the self-righteous concepts of secular humanism disregard the validity of God's commandments. Mainly because they do not believe there is a boundless God who has preeminence over the entire universe. Zuckerman informs:

> *Secular Humanism begins with denial or doubt concerning the existence of anything supernatural - including God - but then goes well beyond that secular stance by positively affirming and valuing the potential of human beings to be kind, enact justice, solve problems, and make the world a better, safer, greener, and more humane place.*[251]

Contrary to God's blueprint, the mindset of Secular Humanism exists throughout the marketplace.

Despite the philosophies of Secular Humanism that infiltrate

---

[250] Matthew 6:33 - King James Version (KJV).

[251] https://www.psychologytoday.com/us/blog/the-secular-life/202002/what-is-secular-humanism.

the marketplace, Christians are holding on to the truth of God's Word. In addition, Christian workers are exuding a wealth of adoration for God in every facet of the marketplace. For example, marketplace Christians are demonstrating their reverence for God in stockholders' and executive board members' meetings. Even entry level Christian workers are reverencing God. As a result, The Lord is fortifying them to resist ungodly strategies. In any given case, the Spirit of God cultivates the speech, thoughts, and actions of every Christian worker who reverence Him.

During the cultivation process, Christians receive greater insight concerning the Master Builder's blueprint for building enduring wealth. Adhering to God's plans, Christian workers are "[growing] in spiritual strength and [becoming] better acquainted with our Lord and Savior Jesus Christ."[252] As Christians grow in spiritual strength, they can stay focused on the Master Builder. Focusing on the Master Builder is key to staying on the path of enduring wealth. One way to stay focus on the Master Builder is to constantly commune with him in prayer.

While communing with the master Builder in prayer, Christians gain strength to resist self-sufficiency. From a Biblical perspective, relying totally on one's own abilities is toxic.

---

[252] 2 Peter 3:18 - Living Bible (TLB).

Furthermore, self-reliance can cultivate the spirit of pride. Pride gives vent to arrogance, self-righteousness, and superiority. In any given case, Proverbs 15:5 informs, "everyone who is proud and arrogant in heart is disgusting and exceedingly offensive to the Lord; Be assured he will not go unpunished."[253] Although the Bible speaks against the disposition of pride, many scholars believe there is a positive form of pride called "self-respect".[254]

Psychologists view self-respect as being a positive form of pride because it is "a reasonable and justifiable sense of one's own worth."[255] However, believers should carefully observe pride under the microscope of God's Word. Why? Because the Bible paints a vivid picture of the devastating effects of pride. Therefore, all Christians must be alert and resist pride. Thomas A. Tarrants informs:

> *It would be easy to conclude that pride is the special problem of those who are rich, powerful, successful, famous, or self-righteous. But that is wrong. [Pride takes different shapes] and forms and affects all of us.*[256]

---

[253] Proverbs 16:5 - Amplified Bible (AMP).

[254] Merriam-Webster Dictionary.

[255] https://www.merriam-webster.com/dictionary/pride.

[256] https://www.cslewisinstitute.org/resources/pride-and-humility/.

Although pride affects all humans, the Master Builder's blueprint reveals the remedy for pride. He speaks clearly in Romans 12:3 saying:

> . . . it is important that [we do not] misinterpret [ourselves] as people who are bringing this goodness to God. No, God brings it all to [us]. The only accurate way to understand ourselves is by what God is and by what he does for us, not by what we are and what we do for him.[257]

Next, in James 4:6, He informs, ". . . God gives strength to the humble but sets himself against the proud and haughty.[258] Therefore, anyone seeking to gain the victory over pride must exercise humility.

The Bible paints a vivid picture of the benefits of walking humbly with God.

> As the Scripture says, God gives strength to the humble but sets himself against the proud and haughty. So, give yourselves humbly to God. Resist the devil and he will flee from you.[259]

Those who walk humble before the Lord are guaranteed strength. In

---

[257] Romans 12:3 - The Message (MSG).

[258] James 4:6 - Living Bible (TLB).

[259] James 4:7 - Living Bible (TLB).

addition to increasing in strength, individuals who walk in "true humility and respect for the Lord [are led] to riches, honor, and long life."[260] Bringing Proverbs 22:4 and Proverbs 3:5-6 together, true humility gives way to trusting the Lord wholeheartedly and respect gives way to acknowledging Him. So, the keys to riches, honor, and long life are humbly walking with God coupled with trusting, respecting, and always acknowledging Him.

While humility and respect lead to riches, honor, and long life; pride leads to destruction. Sadly, individuals who yield to the spirit of pride become spiritually malnourished because they refuse to humbly acknowledge the Bread of Life. In addition, they become spiritually dehydrated because they reject the Living Water. Being spiritually malnourished and dehydrated, a proud individual has a distorted view of God. Having lost focus on the Master Builder, proudful individuals drift into paths that seem right. The Bible explains the paths of proud individuals by saying, "There is a way that seems right to a person, but eventually it ends in death."[261] But since it is not God's will for proudful individuals to perish, He invites them to follow Him on the path of enduring wealth.

To follow the Master Builder on the path of ongoing wealth,

---

[260] Proverbs 22:4 - Living Bible (TLB).

[261] Proverbs 14:12 - GOD'S WORD Translation (GW).

the Christian worker must abandon thinking too high of him or herself and trust the Master Builder. Although Christians encounter circumstances that make an appeal to their propensity to be proudful, Christians must resist the spirit of pride. Instead, Christian workers must always remain humble and trust in the Lord. Notice what the Bible declares in Jeremiah 17:7, "Blessed is the man who trusts in the Lord, and whose hope is the Lord." Trusting God keeps Christian workers from living in the dreary fog of frustration wondering if godly success is possible in the marketplace.

God has never planned for Christian workers to struggle trying to build wealth based on finite strategies. While finite strategies may fulfill the lust of the eyes, the lust of the flesh, and the pride of life, they will never produce enduring wealth. The only way to build enduring wealth is to follow the Master Builder's blueprint. Be aware, building according to the Master Builder's blueprint does not guarantee the believer will be free of temptations. In fact, the Master Builder gives a powerful word of advice, "in the world you have tribulation *and* distress *and* suffering, but be courageous [be confident, be undaunted, be filled with joy]; I have overcome the world."[262] All because of the abiding victory of Christ Jesus, Christians can overcome the temptations of the world.

---

[262] John 16:33 - Amplified Bible (AMP).

The Master Builder gets the glory when Christians overcome the temptations of the world. In addition, the Lord Jesus gets the glory when Christian workers exude bold confidence and live a life of surrender. Living a life of surrender means the Christian worker "[walks] by faith and not by sight" as the Master Builder directs his or her paths. Surrendering also means living life on God's terms – by adhering to His blueprint for building wealth.

Chapter 8
The Master Builder's Blueprint

The full scope of the Master Builder's blueprint for gaining endless wealth exist in the eternal mind of God. Although the Bible reveals aspects of the Master Builder's blueprint, humans still need to receive revelation, ongoing illumination, godly knowledge, godly understanding, and godly wisdom to properly apply God's wealth-building principles. Gaining the capacity to follow God's blueprint is possible by entering a covenant relationship with the Master Builder. In other words, an individual must put off his or her old lifestyle and put on the new lifestyle that produces the fruit of righteousness and holiness.[263]

Putting on the new lifestyle begins with yoking up with the Master Builder. To yoke up with Christ the believer must exercise faith in God and commit to finding rest in Christ alone. At the same time, the individual must be committed to following Christ and building with Him. As a result, the Master Builder empowers the believer to put on the new lifestyle and begin the journey of traveling on the path of enduring wealth. On the path of enduring wealth,

---

[263] Ephesians 4:24 - King James Version (KJV).

believers increase in wealth both spiritually and naturally.

One of the great benefits of being Spiritually wealthy is having godly wisdom for making prudent decisions that produce natural wealth. Natural wealth includes the financial, physical, social, mental, emotional, and other aspects of life. Since God is concerned about every aspect of our lives, He desires for His people to prosper both spiritually and naturally. However, the key to having a constant flow of both spiritual and natural wealth is faithfully following the Master Builder's five wealth building principles: 1) seeking God first in every season of life, 2) trusting the Lord wholeheartedly, 3) always acknowledging the Lord, 4) remembering the Lord is the source of wealth, and 5) glorifying God in every dimension of wealth.

Seeking God first is the essential key to glorifying God in every dimension of wealth. In fact, seeking God first is an act of faith that gives way to complete submission to the mind of God. Also, when a believer seeks God first, he or she is acknowledging the authority of God's Word seen in Isaiah 55:8-9:

> *[God's] thoughts are not [our] thoughts, nor are [our] ways [His] ways. . . For as the heavens are higher than the earth, so are [His] ways higher than [our] ways and [His] thoughts*

than [our] thoughts.[264]

To avoid the snare of leaning to our own understanding, Christians must pursue the thoughts of God by seeking God first.

Having the necessary wisdom to follow the Master Builder's blueprint will always lead to other opportunities for believers to seek Him first. Interestingly, opportunities to seek the mind of God surface during the swift transitions of life. For instance, encountering a sudden decline in customer service, a sudden shift in the economy, or a sudden decrease in profitability growth are opportunities to seek God first. In any given case, when believers seek God first, He will faithfully reveal His glory, give insight, and prosper His people. When God prospers His people, it is for the sole purpose of manifesting His will in the earth.

As God manifest His will in the earth, He work in the lives of marketplace Christians to fulfill a certain facet of His overall plan. While fulfilling His overall plan, God oversees the affairs of His people on an individual level. For example, it is God's will for elected Christian Business owners to assist in local missions while others assist in foreign missions. In effort to set the stage for believers to fulfill their purpose, God will gently guide believers

---

[264] Isaiah 55:8-9 - Amplified Bible (AMP).

through the swift transitions of life. Swift transitions can lead to both pleasant and unpleasant experiences. An unpleasant season that readily comes to mind is a decrease in profitable growth.

Just imagine going for ten years with each year increasing in profitable growth and suddenly things change. For instance, two best friends who are Christians became entrepreneurs just months apart. Both owners have an excellent brand image, great marketing strategies, good organizational structure, a solid financial plan, and both owners effectively use outside resources. In addition, both owners faithfully give to their local churches and are known for contributing to various scholarship programs. However, during the pandemic, both owners experienced a decrease in profitable growth.

Although the decrease in profitable growth is a new season for both owners, before moving forward or just settling for a lack of profitable growth, both business owners pursued God first. While seeking the mind of God, one business owner received instructions from God to assist a specific local mission. But God instructed the other business owner to assist in a specific foreign mission. After the owners moved forward in faith-filled obedience, the Master Builder showed Himself strong on their behalf. God revealed His glory, gave insight, and prospered the two business owners beyond anything they ever imagined.

Christians receive bountiful blessings when they seek God

first. Seeking God first prevents believers from readily leaning to their own understanding. Even when a believer's logic dictates a grim outcome, he or she must seek God first. In the process of seeking God first, there may be times when God appears not to be listening. However, believers must persistently pursue God, trust Him wholeheartedly, and always acknowledge Him.

While traveling on the path of enduring wealth, Christian workers will encounter challenging times. There will be times when Christian managers will face problematic decisions that cause a great deal of discomfort. For example, terminating an employee, managing conflict within the department, and/or the overwhelming impact of working long hours can be incredibly challenging. Nevertheless, the Christian must resist the urge to lean to his or her own understanding. Why? Because leaning to one's own understanding shifts his or her focus from the boundless power of God to the challenges of the workplace.

Focusing on the challenges of the marketplace can cause anger to surface. Although anger is a natural emotion, the Bible warns, "when you are angry, [do not] let it carry you into sin ... or give the devil room to work."[265] To prevent giving the devil room to work, marketplace Christians must trust and acknowledge the Lord

---

[265] Ephesians 4:26-27 - The Voice (VOICE).

in all their ways. When Christians trust and acknowledge the Lord, they resist the propensity to use earthly wisdom. In fact, they rely on the wisdom of God to help them make prudent decisions.

Even entry level Christian workers can use godly wisdom to supersede the expectations of senior workers. For example, entry level Christians will do more than respect office rules, listen to instructions, and follow the dress code, but they will also exude the fruit of the Spirit. Entry level Christians will also work in the spirit of excellence and exemplify integrity without being micromanaged. Furthermore, using godly wisdom, entry level Christian workers will be effective communicators, faithfully attend work, arrive to work on time, and be open to constructive feedback.

The more entry level Christian workers use godly wisdom, the more they prosper both spiritually and naturally. From a spiritual perspective, entry level workers will grow in grace and in the knowledge of God through firsthand experiences in the workplace. God gives them the spiritual fortitude to resist the tactics of the enemy. While resisting the forces of darkness, entry level Christian workers have support from heaven's army. If entry level Christians continue to seek God first, trust in the Lord, and acknowledge Him, they will prosper in a manner that will glorify God.

No matter what capacity Christian workers serve in, trusting and acknowledging the boundless Master Builder always results in a victorious outcome. Since God knows everything, He knows how to direct the paths of faithful followers to fulfill His plan. Despite the complexities of the marketplace, the boundless Master Builder causes Christian workers to prosper in every dimension of wealth. There is absolutely no situation too complexed for the boundless Master Builder. In fact, He allows complex situations to surface so Christian workers will have an opportunity to look unto Him for solutions.

The Master Builder's blueprint reveals solutions full of godly wisdom, knowledge, and understanding. With that thought in mind, His solutions surpass the most innovative technology. The Master Builder's solutions will cause operational managers, middle managers, and senior managers to prosper infinitely beyond their greatest prayers, hopes, or dreams. For example, God's solutions will enable operational managers to implement strategies that will cause every aspect of the production process to manifest God's glory in ways they never imagined. In reference to senior managers, applying God's solutions is the antidote for overcoming the propensity to jump unscrupulously from stage to stage.

Adhering to the Master Builder's blueprint, senior managers will prosper in a godly manner making the atmosphere conducive for God's peace to flow throughout the workplace. As the peace of God reigns, workers on all levels will experience psychological well-being. In addition, God's peace will saturate the innermost being of Christian workers as well as draw non-Christians to Him. The peace of God flowing throughout the workplace will also dismantle the mental and spiritual attacks of the adversary. As a result, the spirit of manipulation and corporate politics will cease and workers on all levels will perpetuate systems that encourage others to release their fullest potential.

Furthermore, the Boundless Master Builder will optimize the strengths of senior managers to fulfill His divine purpose. When senior managers seek, trust, and acknowledge the Master Builder, He shows Himself strong on their behalf. Things that would normally cause senior managers to experience burnout, the Master Builder shifts the situation into a victorious outcome. During divine adjustments, senior managers can gain insight on when to take a vacation. While senior managers are getting the necessary rest, God will work through middle managers and individual contributors to keep the entire company on track. So much so, the senior manager will know - the Master Builder was always at work while he or she was on vacation.

Having no respect of person, the Master Builder will also work on the behalf of middle managers. Despite the various fluctuations in the business, the Master Builder knows how to direct the paths of Christian managers as He reveals supernatural strategies. For example, when Christians who are in middle management trust and acknowledge the Lord as they make tactical decisions, He will reveal strategies that no finite being could ever imagine. Even during conflict resolution, middle managers will receive divine actions that will create a peaceful environment throughout the entire company. In addition, middle managers will gain access to divine strategies that will enlarge the company's territory and build the Kingdom of God at the same time.

If Christians who are in middle management positions trust and acknowledge God, the Master Builder will continue to allow them to prosper in every dimension of wealth. Middle managers will prosper in such a manner their communication will be a demonstration of godly wisdom. Using godly wisdom, middle managers will speak kind words in due season and radiate the love of God while giving employee's feedback on their performance. Furthermore, middle managers will effectively report to upper management in a manner that will help to shape the company's culture for God's glory.

Walking in the divine order of God, middle managers can glorify God as they adjust procedures and priorities to support the vision and philosophy of the business. As spiritually wealthy role models, they will not only be liaisons between upper management and individual contributors, but middle managers will also be a divine connection linking souls to the Master Builder. Winning souls is a labor of love that honors God. As a result, God allows middle managers to prosper both spiritually and naturally. In addition, He strengthens, energizes, and fortifies soul-winning managers to stay yoked up with the Master Builder.

As middle managers stay yoked up with the Master Builder, they receive godly wisdom for moving up the corporate hierarchy. In God's infinite wisdom, He knows how to direct the paths of middle managers so they will not get stuck in limbo. Even if a middle manager is not destined to work in upper management, God knows the perfect lateral move that will expand the manager's perspective. The Master Builder has the perfect plan for keeping middle managers on the path of enduring wealth. The wonderful thing about being on the path of enduring wealth is the Master Builder "gives [Christians] grace and glory. No good thing will he withhold from those who walk along his paths."[266]

Like senior and middle managers, Christian operational managers can walk along God's paths and reap enduring benefits. For example, operational managers who acknowledge the Lord will receive godly wisdom for effectively managing diversity and cultural differences. The Master Builder will enlighten operational managers to see diversity and cultural differences as an opportunity to demonstrate the fruit of the Spirit. He will also show managers how to use cultural differences as an opportunity to win souls for Christ.

Operational managers who seek to win souls in the workplace will receive natural and spiritual blessings that are exceedingly abundantly above anything they ever dreamed possible.

---

[266] Psalm 84:11 - Living Bible (TLB).

From a natural perspective, operational managers will gain access to God's blueprint for implementing truthful processes and practices across the organization. Despite the forces of darkness lurking in the marketplace, God will prosper operational managers as they procure materials, formulate strategies, improve performance, and secure compliance. Operational managers are destined to prosper both spiritually and naturally as they glorify God in the workplace.

The workplace is also an extraordinary place for God to show Himself strong on the behalf of Christians. As God shows Himself strong in the workplace, He uses the complexities of organizational structure to reveal His plan. For instance, He uses competing business practices to highlight the need for spiritual structure and balance. He uses the loss of productivity that happened during the training to direct managers to the One who supplies all the company's needs. He also uses departmental clashes to remind Christian workers to acknowledge the Prince of Peace.

In every situation, the Prince of Peace knows how to work everything together for good. So, instead of struggling to find prudent resolutions, managers can receive council from the God of peace by simply trusting and acknowledging Him. Not just managers, but Christian workers on all levels can reap enduring benefits by trusting and acknowledging the Lord in all their ways. Christians who trust and acknowledge the Lord in all their ways, reap the benefit of God cultivating and empowering them to remain spiritually guided. Although Christians are known for yielding to God's guidance, sometimes Christians lean toward what is known as being a gut reaction. However, the Master Builder's blueprint instructs believers to remain spiritually guided. Therefore, the Holy Spirit guidance should take precedence over any other decision-making style.

Christians who make decisions based on gut reaction or using the list approach must yield to the voice of the Lord. Also, Christians who naturally use collective reasoning must be open to receive guidance from the Master Builder. He is the only One who can reveal if the group's consensus coincides with His plans for building enduring wealth. Regardless of the decision-making style Christians use, they must trust the Lord, acknowledge Him in all their ways, remain humble, and follow His guidance. As a result, He will continue to strengthen, energize, and fortify them until the spiritually guided decision-making style becomes primary.

Christian workers who use the spiritually guided decision-making style will increase in spiritual wealth. In addition, Christian workers will increase in natural wealth as they follow the leading of the Holy Spirit. As Christians prosper, they must continue to always trust and acknowledge the Lord. When believers follow the principles of trusting and acknowledging the Lord, He directs their paths into new dimensions of wealth. In fact, the Master Builder empowers all faith-filled followers to demonstrate the authority of being spiritually wealthy.

Chapter 9
Conclusion

Following the Master Builder's blueprint for building enduring wealth, Christians can "lay up for [themselves] treasures in heaven."[267] While laying up treasures in heaven Christians reap dividends in this present world. However, the final payment for laying up treasures in heaven will be in eternity. But in the meantime, Christians can increase their spiritual wealth while traveling the path of enduring wealth. Having the ability to increase spiritual wealth is a divine benefit given to everyone who receives the Holy Spirit.

Without the Holy Spirit, an individual is powerless and cannot adhere to the principles for building spiritual wealth. Although he or she may possess the riches of this world, he or she is still spiritually poor without the power of the Holy Spirit. Furthermore, without the Holy Spirit humans are driven by "the lust and sensual craving of the flesh and the lust and longing of the eyes and the boastful pride of life [which is] pretentious confidence in

---

[267] Matthew 6:20 - New International Version (NIV).

one's resources or in the stability of earthly things."[268] All of which further compound the horrific effects of "being born in sin." From birth, all humans are spiritually dead and lack the necessary power to break the grip of spiritual poverty.

Breaking the grip of spiritual poverty is the main reason the Master Builder came in the likeness of sinful flesh. He came,

> *. . .to preach Good News to the poor; . . . to heal the brokenhearted and to announce that captives shall be released, and the blind shall see, that the downtrodden shall be freed from their oppressors, and that God is ready to give blessings to all who come to Him.*[269]

Anyone who comes to God, please Him with faith, and accept the plan of salvation – receives freedom from the disgraceful state of spiritual poverty. Miraculously, the moment a believer receives redemption, he or she enters the path of enduring wealth.

At the onset of entering the path of enduring wealth the infinite Master Builder councils all Christians saying, ". . . here is the conclusion of the matter: fear God and keep His commandments,

---

[268] 1 John 2:16 - Amplified Bible (AMP).

[269] Luke 4:18-19 - Living Bible (TLB)

for this is the duty of all mankind."[270] Therefore, on the path of enduring wealth, Christians have an indispensable duty to fear God first. Fearing God is awe-filled worship. Having a heart filled with reverence, worship, and adoration means the believer has "set [his or her mind] on things above, not on earthly things."[271] Also, to reverence God means the Spirit-filled believer loves God so much he or she finds delight in adhering to the Master Builder's commandments.

The commandments of the Lord are instructions for staying on the path of enduring wealth. In fact, the only way a Christian can stay on the path of enduring wealth, he or she must obey the commandments of the Lord. Obeying God's commandments includes:

> *[Loving] the Lord [our] God with all [our heart] and with all [our soul] and with all [our mind]. This is the first and greatest commandment. And the second is like it: '[Loving our] neighbor as [ourselves]. All the Law and the Prophets hang on these two commandments.* (Matthew 22:36-40)[272]

---

[270] Ecclesiastes 12:13 - New International Version (NIV).

[271] Colossians 3:2 - New International Version (NIV).

[272] Matthew 22:36-40 - New International Version (NIV).

The Master Builder's Blueprint for Building Enduring Wealth

Christians can love God and others because the Holy Spirit has poured God's love in their hearts. The love of God miraculously created a new heart. With the new heart, Christians have the power to adhere to the two greatest commandments as well as all the other commandments. In addition, the believer who loves God with all his or her heart, finds pleasure resting in Him, following Him, and building with Him. Having found rest for their soul, Christians peacefully walk by faith looking unto Jesus who is the Author and Finisher of our faith. As believers keep looking unto the Master Builder, He strengthens, energizes, and fortifies Christians to faithfully follow His blueprint.

Following the divine blueprint, believers increase in spiritual and natural wealth. Using spiritual and natural wealth, Christians demonstrate their love for God and other humans in every dimension of wealth. To keep a constant flow of spiritual and natural wealth Christians must practice following the Master Builder's five wealth building principles: 1) seeking God first in every season of life, 2) trusting the Lord wholeheartedly, 3) always acknowledging the Lord, 4) remembering the Lord is the source of wealth, and 5) glorifying God in every dimension of wealth. As a result, the boundless Master Builder faithfully reveals His glory, gives insight, and prospers faith-filled followers on the path of enduring wealth.

On the path of enduring wealth, Christians are constantly growing in grace and in the knowledge of the Lord Jesus Christ. As

Christians faithfully follow the Lord Jesus, they constantly increase in godly knowledge, godly understanding, and godly wisdom. Also, following Jesus, Christians manifest the Fruit of the Spirit as they diligently practice spiritual discipline and balance. Amazingly, while faithfully following the Master Builder, Christians will eventually transition out of time over into eternity and "so shall we ever be with the Lord."[273] In the presence of the Lord, we will see the great riches and enduring wealth that God promised:

> *. . . just as it is written [in Scripture], things which [our eyes have] not seen and [our ears have] not heard, and which have not entered the heart of [humans], all that God has prepared for those who love Him - who hold Him in affectionate reverence, who obey Him, and who gratefully recognize the benefits that He has bestowed.*[274]

---

[273] 1 Thessalonians 4:17 - King James Version (KJV).

[274] 1 Corinthians 2:9 - Amplified Bible (AMP).

Works Cited

"Amplified Bible (AMP) - - 1 Corinthians 2:9." Bible Gateway, The Lockman Foundation, 2015, www.biblegateway.com. Accessed 13 Nov. 2023.

"Amplified Bible (AMP) - - 2 Corinthians 5:17." Bible Gateway, The Lockman Foundation, 2015, www.biblegateway.com. Accessed **9 Sept. 2024**.

"Amplified Bible (AMP) - - 2 Corinthians 5:21." Bible Gateway, The Lockman Foundation, 2015, www.biblegateway.com. Accessed 13 Nov. 2023.

"Amplified Bible (AMP) - - 1 John 2:16-17." Bible Gateway, The Lockman Foundation, 2015, www.biblegateway.com. Accessed **9 Sept. 2024**.

"Amplified Bible (AMP) - - Ecclesiastes 3:1a." Bible Gateway, The Lockman Foundation, 2015, www.biblegateway.com. Accessed 13 Nov. 2023.

"Amplified Bible (AMP) - - Genesis 1:3-5." Bible Gateway, The Lockman Foundation, 2015, www.biblegateway.com. Accessed **10 Sept. 2024**.

"Amplified Bible (AMP) - - Genesis 1:24." Bible Gateway, The Lockman Foundation, 2015, www.biblegateway.com.

Accessed 13 Nov. 2023.

"Amplified Bible (AMP) - - Genesis 2:7." Bible Gateway, The Lockman Foundation, 2015, www.biblegateway.com. Accessed **10 Sept. 2024**.

"Amplified Bible (AMP) - - Genesis 6:5-6." Bible Gateway, The Lockman Foundation, 2015, www.biblegateway.com. Accessed **9 Sept. 2024**.

"Amplified Bible (AMP) - - Genesis 11:8." Bible Gateway, The Lockman Foundation, 2015, www.biblegateway.com. Accessed **10 Sept. 2024**.

"Amplified Bible (AMP) - - Hebrews 11:1, 3, 6." Bible Gateway, The Lockman Foundation, 2015, www.biblegateway.com. Accessed 13 Nov. 2023.

"Amplified Bible (AMP) - - Isaiah 40:12; 45:12." Bible Gateway, The Lockman Foundation, 2015, www.biblegateway.com. Accessed 13 Nov. 2023.

"Amplified Bible (AMP) - - Isaiah 46:10; Isaiah 55:8-9." Bible Gateway, The Lockman Foundation, 2015, www.biblegateway.com. Accessed **10 Sept. 2024**.

"Amplified Bible (AMP) - - John 15:4." Bible Gateway, The Lockman Foundation, 2015, www.biblegateway.com. Accessed 13 Nov. 2023.

"Amplified Bible (AMP) - - John 16:33." Bible Gateway, The Lockman Foundation, 2015, www.biblegateway.com. Accessed **10 Sept. 2024**.

"Amplified Bible (AMP) - - Joshua 21:44." Bible Gateway, The Lockman Foundation, 2015, www.biblegateway.com. Accessed 13 Nov. 2023.

"Amplified Bible (AMP) - - Joshua 22:1, 2, 4, 7, 8." Bible Gateway, The Lockman Foundation, 2015, www.biblegateway.com. Accessed 10 Sept. 2024.

"Amplified Bible (AMP) - - Jude 20." Bible Gateway, The Lockman Foundation, 2015, www.biblegateway.com. Accessed 13 Nov. 2023.

"Amplified Bible (AMP) - - Lamentations 3:23." Bible Gateway, The Lockman Foundation, 2015, www.biblegateway.com. Accessed **10 Sept. 2024**.

"Amplified Bible (AMP) - - Matthew 11:28-30." Bible Gateway, The Lockman Foundation, 2015, www.biblegateway.com. Accessed **9 Sept. 2024**.

"Amplified Bible (AMP) - - Matthew 14:30." Bible Gateway, The Lockman Foundation, 2015, www.biblegateway.com. Accessed 13 Nov. 2023.

"Amplified Bible (AMP) - - Matthew 23:4." Bible Gateway, The

Lockman Foundation, 2015, www.biblegateway.com. Accessed **9 Sept. 2024**.

"Amplified Bible (AMP) - - Philippians 3:8-9." Bible Gateway, The Lockman Foundation, 2015, www.biblegateway.com. Accessed 13 Nov. 2023.

"Amplified Bible (AMP) - - Philippians 4:12-13." Bible Gateway, The Lockman Foundation, 2015, www.biblegateway.com. Accessed **10 Sept. 2024**.

"Amplified Bible (AMP) - - Proverbs 3:6." Bible Gateway, The Lockman Foundation, 2015, www.biblegateway.com. Accessed 13 Nov. 2023.

"Amplified Bible (AMP) - - Proverbs 16:5." Bible Gateway, The Lockman Foundation, 2015, www.biblegateway.com. Accessed 13 Nov. 2023.

"Amplified Bible (AMP) - - Psalm 34:19." Bible Gateway, The Lockman Foundation, 2015, www.biblegateway.com. Accessed 13 Nov. 2023.

"Amplified Bible (AMP) - - Psalm 73:2-3." Bible Gateway, The Lockman Foundation, 2015, www.biblegateway.com. Accessed 13 Nov. 2023.

"Amplified Bible (AMP) - - Psalm 74:17." Bible Gateway, The Lockman Foundation, 2015, www.biblegateway.com.

Accessed 13 Nov. 2023.

"Amplified Bible (AMP) - - Psalm 139:1-6." Bible Gateway, The Lockman Foundation, 2015, www.biblegateway.com. Accessed **10 Sept. 2024**.

"Amplified Bible (AMP) - - Revelation 1:8." Bible Gateway, The Lockman Foundation, 2015, www.biblegateway.com. Accessed **10 Sept. 2024**.

"Amplified Bible (AMP) - - Titus 2:12." Bible Gateway, The Lockman Foundation, 2015, www.biblegateway.com. Accessed 13 Nov. 2023.

"Amplified Bible, Classic Edition (AMPC) - - 1 Corinthians 15:58." Bible Gateway, The Lockman Foundation, 1987, www.biblegateway.com. Accessed 13 Nov. 2023.

"Amplified Bible, Classic Edition (AMPC) - - Genesis 2:7, 19-20." Bible Gateway, The Lockman Foundation, 1987, www.biblegateway.com. Accessed **10 Sept. 2024**.

"Amplified Bible, Classic Edition (AMPC) - - Matthew 21:22." Bible Gateway, The Lockman Foundation, 1987, www.biblegateway.com. Accessed **9 Sept. 2024**.

Avery, Kim. *The Prayer Powered Entrepreneur*. Morgan James Publishing, 2020, Kindle Edition, p. 45.

Benner, Jeff A. "Definition of Hebrew Names: Noah: AHRC."

Definition of Hebrew Names: Noah | AHRC, 2022,
www.ancient-hebrew.org/names/Noah.htm. Accessed 13
Nov. 2023.

Bradley, Anne, and Art Lindsley, editors. *For the Least of These.*
Zondervan, 2014, Kindle Edition, pp. 60-61.

Calhoun, Adele Ahlberg. *Invitations from God: Accepting God's
Offer to Rest, Weep, Forgive, Wait, Remember and More.*
InterVarsity Press, 2011, Kindle Edition, p. 9.

"Contemporary English Version (CEV) - - 2 Peter 1:3-4." Bible
Gateway, American Bible Society, 1995,
www.biblegateway.com. Accessed 13 Nov. 2023.

"Contemporary English Version (CEV) - - Lamentations 3:22."
Bible Gateway, American Bible Society, 1995,
www.biblegateway.com. Accessed 13 Nov. 2023.

"Contemporary English Version (CEV) - - Psalm 147:4." Bible
Gateway, American Bible Society, 1995,
www.biblegateway.com. Accessed **10 Sept. 2024**.

"Contemporary English Version (CEV) - - Psalm 33:9." Bible
Gateway, American Bible Society, 1995,
www.biblegateway.com. Accessed 13 Nov. 2023.

"Darby Translation (DARBY) - - Ephesians 6:18." Bible Gateway,
Public Domain, 2024, www.biblegateway.com. Accessed **10**

Sept. 2024.

"Darby Translation (DARBY) - - Genesis 1:1, 7-8." Bible Gateway, Public Domain, 2024, www.biblegateway.com. Accessed **10 Sept. 2024**.

"Darby Translation (DARBY) - - Psalm 147:5." Bible Gateway, Public Domain, 2024, www.biblegateway.com. Accessed **9 Sept. 2024**.

DeVries, Simon J. "Time, Meaning of - Holman Bible Dictionary - ." *StudyLight.Org*, Broadman & Holman, 1991, www.studylight.org/dictionaries/eng/hbd/t/time-meaning-of.html. Accessed 13 Nov. 2023.

"Easy-to-Read Version (ERV) - - Daniel 6:10-28." Bible Gateway, by Bible League International, 2006, www.biblegateway.com. Accessed 13 Nov. 2023.

"Easy-to-Read Version (ERV) - - Genesis 2:17." Bible Gateway, by Bible League International, 2006, www.biblegateway.com. Accessed 13 Nov. 2023.

"Easy-to-Read Version (ERV) - Genesis 3:21." Bible Gateway, by Bible League International, 2006, www.biblegateway.com. Accessed **10 Sept. 2024**.

"Easy-to-Read Version (ERV) - - Jeremiah 23:24." Bible Gateway, by Bible League International, 2006, www.biblegateway.com. Accessed **10 Sept. 2024.**

"Easy-to-Read Version (ERV) - - Job 26:7." Bible Gateway, by Bible League International, 2006, www.biblegateway.com. Accessed **9 Sept. 2024.**

"Easy-to-Read Version (ERV) - - Job 38:4-6." Bible Gateway, by Bible League International, 2006, www.biblegateway.com. Accessed **10 Sept. 2024.**

"Easy-to-Read Version (ERV) - - John 15:12." Bible Gateway, by Bible League International, 2006, www.biblegateway.com. Accessed 13 Nov. 2023.

"English Standard Version (ESV) - - Genesis 1:11." Bible Gateway, Crossway Bibles, a publishing ministry of Good News Publishers, 2001, www.biblegateway.com. Accessed 13 Nov. 2023.

"English Standard Version (ESV) - - Genesis 1:14-16." Bible Gateway, Crossway Bibles, a publishing ministry of Good News Publishers, 2001, www.biblegateway.com. Accessed **10 Sept. 2024.**

"English Standard Version (ESV) - - Proverbs 8:29." Bible Gateway, Crossway Bibles, a publishing ministry of Good News Publishers, 2001, www.biblegateway.com. Accessed 13 Nov. 2023.

"English Standard Version (ESV) - - Psalm 19:1, 3." Bible Gateway, Crossway Bibles, a publishing ministry of Good News Publishers, 2001, www.biblegateway.com. Accessed **10 Sept. 2024**.

Galli, Mark, and Ted Olsen. *131 Christians Everyone Should Know*. Broadman & Holman, 2000, Kindle Edition, p. 99.

"GOD'S WORD Translation (GW) - - Proverbs 14:12." Bible Gateway, God's Word to the Nations Mission Society, 2020, www.biblegateway.com. Accessed 13 Nov. 2023.

"Good News Translation (GNT) - - Ephesians 1:18." Bible Gateway, American Bible Society, 1992, www.biblegateway.com. Accessed 13 Nov. 2023.

"Good News Translation (GNT) - - Ezekiel 36:26-27." Bible Gateway, American Bible Society, 1992, www.biblegateway.com. Accessed **9 Sept. 2024**.

"Good News Translation (GNT) - - Genesis 1:27." Bible Gateway, American Bible Society, 1992, www.biblegateway.com. Accessed 13 Nov. 2023.

"Good News Translation (GNT) - - Philippians 1:9." Bible Gateway, American Bible Society, 1992, www.biblegateway.com. Accessed 13 Nov. 2023.

"Good News Translation (GNT) - - Psalms 90:2." Bible Gateway,

American Bible Society, 1992, www.biblegateway.com. Accessed 13 Nov. 2023.

"Good News Translation (GNT) - - Romans 15:13." Bible Gateway, American Bible Society, 1992, www.biblegateway.com. Accessed 13 Nov. 2023.

"Holman Christian Standard Bible (HCSB) - - 2 Timothy 3:12." Bible Gateway, Holman Bible Publishers, 2009, www.biblegateway.com. Accessed 13 Nov. 2023.

"International Children's Bible (ICB) - - Genesis 1:1-31." Bible Gateway, Thomas Nelson, 2015, www.biblegateway.com. Accessed **10 Sept. 2024.**

"International Children's Bible (ICB) - - Genesis 2:1-3; 7, 18-25." Bible Gateway, Thomas Nelson, 2015, www.biblegateway.com. Accessed **10 Sept. 2024.**

Isaiah 40:12 Commentaries: Who Has Measured the Waters in the Hollow of His Hand, and Marked off the Heavens by the Span, and Calculated the Dust of the Earth by the Measure and Weighed the Mountains in a Balance and the Hills in a Pair of Scales? biblehub.com/commentaries/Isaiah/40-12.htm. Accessed 14 Nov. 2023.

"J. B. Phillips New Testament (PHILLIPS) - - 1 Corinthians 2:14-16." Bible Gateway, The Archbishops' Council of the

Church of England, 1972, www.biblegateway.com. Accessed 13 Nov. 2023.

"J. B. Phillips New Testament (PHILLIPS) - - Philippians 4:6-7." Bible Gateway, The Archbishops' Council of the Church of England, 1972, www.biblegateway.com. Accessed **10 Sept. 2024**.

"J. B. Phillips New Testament (PHILLIPS) - - Romans 5:12-14." Bible Gateway, The Archbishops' Council of the Church of England, 1972, www.biblegateway.com. Accessed **10 Sept. 2024**.

"J. B. Phillips New Testament (PHILLIPS) - - Romans 8:5-8." Bible Gateway, The Archbishops' Council of the Church of England, 1972, www.biblegateway.com. Accessed 13 Nov. 2023.

"Jubilee Bible 2000 (JUB) - - Psalm 8:6-8." Bible Gateway, Ransom Press International, 2020, www.biblegateway.com. Accessed 13 Nov. 2023.

"King James Version (KJV) - - 1 John 2:16." Bible Gateway, Public Domain, 2023, www.biblegateway.com. Accessed 13 Nov. 2023.

"King James Version (KJV) - - 1 John 4:20." Bible Gateway, Public Domain, 2023, www.biblegateway.com. Accessed **9 Sept.**

2024.

"King James Version (KJV) - - 1 Thessalonians 4:17." Bible Gateway, Public Domain, 2023, www.biblegateway.com. Accessed 13 Nov. 2023.

"King James Version (KJV) - - 1 Peter 2:5, 9." Bible Gateway, Public Domain, 2023, www.biblegateway.com. Accessed **9 Sept. 2024**.

"King James Version (KJV) - - Acts 17:28." Bible Gateway, Public Domain, 2023, www.biblegateway.com. Accessed **10 Sept. 2024**.

"King James Version (KJV) - - Colossians 3:2." Bible Gateway, Public Domain, 2023, www.biblegateway.com. Accessed 13 Nov. 2023.

"King James Version (KJV) - - Daniel 1:8." Bible Gateway, Public Domain, 2023, www.biblegateway.com. Accessed 13 Nov. 2023.

"King James Version (KJV) - - Daniel 2:21." Bible Gateway, Public Domain, 2023, www.biblegateway.com. Accessed **10 Sept. 2024**.

"King James Version (KJV) - - Ephesians 3:2-6." Bible Gateway, Public Domain, 2023, www.biblegateway.com. Accessed **9 Sept. 2024**.

"King James Version (KJV) - - Ephesians 4:24." Bible Gateway, Public Domain, 2023, www.biblegateway.com. Accessed **10 Sept. 2024**.

"King James Version (KJV) - - Genesis 1:14." Bible Gateway, Public Domain, 2023, www.biblegateway.com. Accessed 13 Nov. 2023.

"King James Version (KJV) - - Genesis 2:16-17." Bible Gateway, Public Domain, 2023, www.biblegateway.com. Accessed **10 Sept. 2024**.

"King James Version (KJV) - - Haggai 2:8." Bible Gateway, Public Domain, 2023, www.biblegateway.com. Accessed 13 Nov. 2023.

"King James Version (KJV) - - Hebrews 11:6." Bible Gateway, Public Domain, 2023, www.biblegateway.com. Accessed 13 Nov. 2023.

"King James Version (KJV) - - Hebrews 13:8." Bible Gateway, Public Domain, 2023, www.biblegateway.com. Accessed **9 Sept. 2024**.

"King James Version (KJV) - - Isaiah 46:10." Bible Gateway, Public Domain, 2023, www.biblegateway.com. Accessed 13 Nov. 2023.

"King James Version (KJV) - - Isaiah 55:8." Bible Gateway, Public

Domain, 2023, www.biblegateway.com. Accessed 13 Nov. 2023.

"King James Version (KJV) - - James 1:17; 4:10." Bible Gateway, Public Domain, 2023, www.biblegateway.com. Accessed **10 Sept. 2024**.

"King James Version (KJV) - - James 3:17." Bible Gateway, Public Domain, 2023, www.biblegateway.com. Accessed 13 Nov. 2023.

"King James Version (KJV) - - James 4:10." Bible Gateway, Public Domain, 2023, www.biblegateway.com. Accessed **10 Sept. 2024**.

"King James Version (KJV) - - Jeremiah 17:9." Bible Gateway, Public Domain, 2023, www.biblegateway.com. Accessed **9 Sept. 2024**.

"King James Version (KJV) - - John 14:23." Bible Gateway, Public Domain, 2023, www.biblegateway.com. Accessed 13 Nov. 2023.

"King James Version (KJV) - - Matthew 6:19-21, 33." Bible Gateway, Public Domain, 2023, www.biblegateway.com. Accessed 13 Nov. 2023.

King James Version (KJV) - - Matthew 11:28-29." Bible Gateway,

Public Domain, 2023, www.biblegateway.com. Accessed **10 Sept. 2024**.

"King James Version (KJV) - - Numbers 23:19." Bible Gateway, Public Domain, 2023, www.biblegateway.com. Accessed 13 Nov. 2023.

"King James Version (KJV) - - Proverbs 3:5-6." Bible Gateway, Public Domain, 2023, www.biblegateway.com. Accessed 13 Nov. 2023.

"King James Version (KJV) - - Proverbs 4:7." Bible Gateway, Public Domain, 2023, www.biblegateway.com. Accessed 13 Nov. 2023.

"King James Version (KJV) - - Proverbs 9:10a." Bible Gateway, Public Domain, 2023, www.biblegateway.com. Accessed **10 Sept. 2024**.

"King James Version (KJV) - - Psalm 19:1." Bible Gateway, Public Domain, 2023, www.biblegateway.com. Accessed 13 Nov. 2023.

"King James Version (KJV) - - Psalm 24:1." Bible Gateway, Public Domain, 2023, www.biblegateway.com. Accessed **10 Sept. 2024**.

"King James Version (KJV) - - Psalm 37:7a." Bible Gateway, Public Domain, 2023, www.biblegateway.com. Accessed **9 Sept.**

2024.

"King James Version (KJV) - - Psalm 90:4." Bible Gateway, Public Domain, 2023, www.biblegateway.com. Accessed **10 Sept. 2024**.

"King James Version (KJV) - - Psalm 119:89." Bible Gateway, Public Domain, 2023, www.biblegateway.com. Accessed 13 Nov. 2023.

"King James Version (KJV) - - Romans 2:11." Bible Gateway, Public Domain, 2023, www.biblegateway.com. Accessed 13 Nov. 2023.

"King James Version (KJV) - - Romans 5:3-5." Bible Gateway, Public Domain, 2023, www.biblegateway.com. Accessed 13 Nov. 2023.

"King James Version (KJV) - - Romans 8:4." Bible Gateway, Public Domain, 2023, www.biblegateway.com. Accessed 9 Sept. 2024.

"King James Version (KJV) - - Romans 13:14." Bible Gateway, Public Domain, 2023, www.biblegateway.com. Accessed **9 Sept. 2024**.

"KJV Dictionary Definition: Time." Edited by B Staggs, *AV1611.Com*, 2023, av1611.com/kjbp/kjv-dictionary/time.html. Accessed 13 Nov. 2023.

"Living Bible (TLB) - - 2 Peter 1:5; 3:18." Bible Gateway, Thomas Nelson, 1982, www.biblegateway.com. Accessed 13 Nov. 2023.

"Living Bible (TLB) - - Acts 16:16-36." Bible Gateway, Thomas Nelson, 1982, www.biblegateway.com. Accessed 13 Nov. 2023.

"Living Bible (TLB) - - Ephesians 1:4-5." Bible Gateway, Thomas Nelson, 1982, www.biblegateway.com. Accessed 13 Nov. 2023.

"Living Bible (TLB) - - Ephesians 3:20." Bible Gateway, Thomas Nelson, 1982, www.biblegateway.com. Accessed 13 Nov. 2023.

"Living Bible (TLB) - - Ezekiel 36:26-27." Bible Gateway, Thomas Nelson, 1982, www.biblegateway.com. Accessed 13 Nov. 2023.

"Living Bible (TLB) - - Genesis 1:10." Bible Gateway, Thomas Nelson, 1982, www.biblegateway.com. Accessed **10 Sept. 2024**.

"Living Bible (TLB) - - Genesis 2:9." Bible Gateway, Thomas Nelson, 1982, www.biblegateway.com. Accessed **10 Sept. 2024**.

"Living Bible (TLB) - - Genesis 11:3-4." Bible Gateway, Thomas

Nelson, 1982, www.biblegateway.com. Accessed **10 Sept. 2024**.

"Living Bible (TLB) - - Hebrews 11:1." Bible Gateway, Thomas Nelson, 1982, www.biblegateway.com. Accessed **9 Sept. 2024**.

"Living Bible (TLB) - - Hebrews 11:6." Bible Gateway, Thomas Nelson, 1982, www.biblegateway.com. Accessed 13 Nov. 2023.

"Living Bible (TLB) - - James 2:19." Bible Gateway, Thomas Nelson, 1982, www.biblegateway.com. Accessed **9 Sept. 2024**.

"Living Bible (TLB) - - James 4:6-7." Bible Gateway, Thomas Nelson, 1982, www.biblegateway.com. Accessed 13 Nov. 2023.

"Living Bible (TLB) - - Jeremiah 9:23-24." Bible Gateway, Thomas Nelson, 1982, www.biblegateway.com. Accessed 13 Nov. 2023.

"Living Bible (TLB) - - Luke 4:18-19." Bible Gateway, Thomas Nelson, 1982, www.biblegateway.com. Accessed 13 Nov. 2023.

"Living Bible (TLB) - - Matthew 7:12." Bible Gateway, Thomas Nelson, 1982, www.biblegateway.com. Accessed 13 Nov.

2023.

"Living Bible (TLB) - - Philippians 2:13." Bible Gateway, Thomas Nelson, 1982, www.biblegateway.com. Accessed 13 Nov. 2023.

"Living Bible (TLB) - - Proverbs 22:4." Bible Gateway, Thomas Nelson, 1982, www.biblegateway.com. Accessed 13 Nov. 2023.

"Living Bible (TLB) - - Psalm 34:19." Bible Gateway, Thomas Nelson, 1982, www.biblegateway.com. Accessed 13 Nov. 2023.

"Living Bible (TLB) - - Psalm 84:11." Bible Gateway, Thomas Nelson, 1982, www.biblegateway.com. Accessed **10 Sept. 2024**.

"Living Bible (TLB) - - Proverbs 22:4." Bible Gateway, Thomas Nelson, 1982, www.biblegateway.com. Accessed **10 Sept. 2024**.

"Living Bible (TLB) - - Psalm 34:19; Psalm84:11." Bible Gateway, Thomas Nelson, 1982, www.biblegateway.com. Accessed **10 Sept. 2024**.

"Living Bible (TLB) - - Psalm 90:2." Bible Gateway, Thomas Nelson, 1982, www.biblegateway.com. Accessed **9 Sept. 2024**.

Matthew 11 Ellicott's Commentary for English Readers, 2004, biblehub.com/commentaries/Ellicott/Matthew/11.htm. Accessed 13 Nov. 2023.

Montgomery, John Warwick, and Gene Edward Veith, editors. *Where Christ Is Present: A Theology for All Seasons on the 500th Anniversary of the Reformation.* New Reformation Publications, 2015, Kindle Edition, pp. 220-221.

"New International Version (NIV) - - 1 Corinthians 10:13." Bible Gateway, Public Domain, 2023, www.biblegateway.com. Accessed 13 Nov. 2023.

"New International Version (NIV) - - 2 Peter 3:18." Bible Gateway, Public Domain, 2023, www.biblegateway.com. Accessed 13 Nov. 2023.

"New International Version (NIV) - - Acts 18:1-3; Colossians 3:2." Bible Gateway, Public Domain, 2023, www.biblegateway.com. Accessed 13 Nov. 2023.

"New International Version (NIV) - - Colossians 3:2." Bible Gateway, Public Domain, 2023, www.biblegateway.com. Accessed **9 Sept. 2024.**

"New International Version (NIV) - - Deuteronomy 8:18." Bible Gateway, Public Domain, 2023, www.biblegateway.com. Accessed **10 Sept. 2024.**

"New International Version (NIV) - - Ecclesiastes 3:11." Bible Gateway, Public Domain, 2023, www.biblegateway.com. Accessed **10 Sept. 2024**.

"New International Version (NIV) - - Ecclesiastes 12:13." Bible Gateway, Public Domain, 2023, www.biblegateway.com. Accessed **10 Sept. 2024**.

"New International Version (NIV) - - Ephesians 2:10." Bible Gateway, Public Domain, 2023, www.biblegateway.com. Accessed 13 Nov. 2023.

"New International Version (NIV) - - Galatians 5:22-23." Bible Gateway, Public Domain, 2023, www.biblegateway.com. Accessed **10 Sept. 2024**.

"New International Version (NIV) - - Genesis 1:3, 4, 9, 12." Bible Gateway, Public Domain, 2023, www.biblegateway.com. Accessed 13 Nov. 2023.

"New International Version (NIV) - - Genesis 3:7." Bible Gateway, Public Domain, 2023, www.biblegateway.com. Accessed **10 Sept. 2024**.

"New International Version (NIV) - - Genesis 8:22." Bible Gateway, Public Domain, 2023, www.biblegateway.com. Accessed **10 Sept. 2024**.

"New International Version (NIV) - - Genesis 11:4, 8-9." Bible

Gateway, Public Domain, 2023, www.biblegateway.com. Accessed 13 Nov. 2023.

"New International Version (NIV) - - Hebrews 11:6." Bible Gateway, Public Domain, 2023, www.biblegateway.com. Accessed 13 Nov. 2023.

"New International Version (NIV) - - Isaiah 6:2-3; 25:1." Bible Gateway, Public Domain, 2023, www.biblegateway.com. Accessed **10 Sept. 2024**.

"New International Version (NIV) - - Isaiah 32:17-18." Bible Gateway, Public Domain, 2023, www.biblegateway.com. Accessed 13 Nov. 2023

"New International Version (NIV) - - Isaiah 40:26." Bible Gateway, Public Domain, 2023, www.biblegateway.com. Accessed **10 Sept. 2024**.

"New International Version (NIV) - - Isaiah 44:24." Bible Gateway, Public Domain, 2023, www.biblegateway.com. Accessed 13 Nov. 2023

"New International Version (NIV) - - James 1:5-7." Bible Gateway, Public Domain, 2023, www.biblegateway.com. Accessed **10 Sept. 2024**.

"New International Version (NIV) - - James 3:15." Bible Gateway, Public Domain, 2023, www.biblegateway.com. Accessed **10**

Sept. 2024.

"New International Version (NIV) - - James 2:19." Bible Gateway, Public Domain, 2023, www.biblegateway.com. Accessed 13 Nov. 2023.

"New International Version (NIV) - - James 3:15." Bible Gateway, Public Domain, 2023, www.biblegateway.com. Accessed 13 Nov. 2023.

"New International Version (NIV) - - Jeremiah 29:11." Bible Gateway, Public Domain, 2023, www.biblegateway.com. Accessed 13 Nov. 2023.

"New International Version (NIV) - - John 3:9." Bible Gateway, Public Domain, 2023, www.biblegateway.com. Accessed 13 Nov. 2023.

"New International Version (NIV) - - John 16:32, 33." Bible Gateway, Public Domain, 2023, www.biblegateway.com. Accessed **10 Sept. 2024**.

"New International Version (NIV) - - Jude 1:20." Bible Gateway, Public Domain, 2023, www.biblegateway.com. Accessed 13 Nov. 2023.

"New International Version (NIV) - - Mark 8:36." Bible Gateway, Public Domain, 2023, www.biblegateway.com. Accessed 13 Nov. 2023.

"New International Version (NIV) - - Matthew 5:45." Bible Gateway, Public Domain, 2023, www.biblegateway.com. Accessed **10 Sept. 2024**.

"New International Version (NIV) - - Matthew 6:20." Bible Gateway, Public Domain, 2023, www.biblegateway.com. Accessed 13 Nov. 2023.

"New International Version (NIV) - - Matthew 7:7-8." Bible Gateway, Public Domain, 2023, www.biblegateway.com. Accessed **10 Sept. 2024**.

"New International Version (NIV) - - Matthew 11:28-30." Bible Gateway, Public Domain, 2023, www.biblegateway.com. Accessed **9 Sept. 2024**.

"New International Version (NIV) - - Matthew 22:36-40." Bible Gateway, Public Domain, 2023, www.biblegateway.com. Accessed **9 Sept. 2024**.

"New International Version (NIV) - - Philippians 3:5." Bible Gateway, Public Domain, 2023, www.biblegateway.com. Accessed 13 Nov. 2023.

"New International Version (NIV) - - Philippians 4:7." Bible Gateway, Public Domain, 2023, www.biblegateway.com. Accessed **10 Sept. 2024**.

"New International Version (NIV) - - Philippians 4:19." Bible

Gateway, Public Domain, 2023, www.biblegateway.com. Accessed 13 Nov. 2023.

"New International Version (NIV) - - Proverbs 3:5-6." Bible Gateway, Public Domain, 2023, www.biblegateway.com. Accessed 13 Nov. 2023.

"New International Version (NIV) - - Psalm 107:9." Bible Gateway, Public Domain, 2023, www.biblegateway.com. Accessed 13 Nov. 2023.

"New International Version (NIV) - - Romans 8:5-8." Bible Gateway, Public Domain, 2023, www.biblegateway.com. Accessed 13 Nov. 2023.

"New Century Version (NCV) - - Hebrews 11:3." Bible Gateway, Thomas Nelson, 2005, www.biblegateway.com. Accessed 13 Nov. 2023.

"New Century Version (NCV) - - Genesis 6:8-9." Bible Gateway, Thomas Nelson, 2005, www.biblegateway.com. Accessed 13 Nov. 2023.

"New Century Version (NCV) - - Genesis 8:4." Bible Gateway, Thomas Nelson, 2005, www.biblegateway.com. Accessed **10 Sept. 2024**.

"New Century Version (NCV) - - Isaiah 45:3." Bible Gateway, Thomas Nelson, 2005, www.biblegateway.com. Accessed

13 Nov. 2023.

"New English Translation (NET) - - Genesis 2:7." Bible Gateway, Biblical Studies Press, L.L.C. http://netbible.com, 2017, www.biblegateway.com. Accessed **10 Sept. 2024**.

"New King James Version (NKJV) - - 2 Corinthians 5:7." Bible Gateway, Thomas Nelson, 1982, www.biblegateway.com. Accessed **9 Sept. 2024**.

"New King James Version (NKJV) - - Colossians 3:2." Bible Gateway, Thomas Nelson, 1982, www.biblegateway.com. Accessed **9 Sept. 2024**.

"New King James Version (NKJV) - - Isaiah 11:10." Bible Gateway, Thomas Nelson, 1982, www.biblegateway.com. Accessed **10 Sept. 2024**.

"New King James Version (NKJV) - - Isaiah 16:5." Bible Gateway, Thomas Nelson, 1982, www.biblegateway.com. Accessed 13 Nov. 2023.

"New King James Version (NKJV) - - Isaiah 32:17-18." Bible Gateway, Thomas Nelson, 1982, www.biblegateway.com. Accessed **10 Sept. 2024**.

"New King James Version (NKJV) - - Isaiah 35:1-2, 8." Bible Gateway, Thomas Nelson, 1982, www.biblegateway.com. Accessed 13 Nov. 2023.

"New King James Version (NKJV) - - Philippians 4:6-7." Bible Gateway, Thomas Nelson, 1982, www.biblegateway.com. Accessed 13 Nov. 2023.

"New King James Version (NKJV) - - Revelation 20:1–3." Bible Gateway, Thomas Nelson, 1982, www.biblegateway.com. Accessed 13 Nov. 2023.

"New King James Version (NKJV) - - Titus 2:14." Bible Gateway, Thomas Nelson, 1982, www.biblegateway.com. Accessed **9 Sept. 2024**.

"New Life Version (NLV) - - Genesis 6:8-9." Bible Gateway, Barbour Publishing, Inc, 2003, www.biblegateway.com. Accessed **10 Sept. 2024**.

"New Life Version (NLV) - - Genesis 8:4." Bible Gateway, Barbour Publishing, Inc, 2003, www.biblegateway.com. Accessed **10 Sept. 2024**.

"New Life Version (NLV) - - Isaiah 45:3." Bible Gateway, Barbour Publishing, Inc, 2003, www.biblegateway.com. Accessed **10 Sept. 2024**

"New Living Translation (NLT) - - Deuteronomy 5:33." Bible Gateway, Tyndale House Publishers, 2015, www.biblegateway.com. Accessed **10 Sept. 2024**.

"New Living Translation (NLT) - - Deuteronomy 6:11." Bible Gateway, Tyndale House Publishers, 2015, www.biblegateway.com. Accessed 13 Nov. 2023.

"New Living Translation (NLT) - - Genesis 3:7, 23." Bible Gateway, Tyndale House Publishers, 2015, www.biblegateway.com. Accessed 13 Nov. 2023

"New Living Translation (NLT) - - Genesis 6:5, 14, 22." Bible Gateway, Tyndale House Publishers, 2015, www.biblegateway.com. Accessed **10 Sept. 2024**.

"New Living Translation (NLT) - - John 16: 33." Bible Gateway, Tyndale House Publishers, 2015, www.biblegateway.com. Accessed 13 Nov. 2023.

"New Living Translation (NLT) - - Proverbs 3:6." Bible Gateway, Tyndale House Publishers, 2015, www.biblegateway.com. Accessed 13 Nov. 2023.

"New Living Translation (NLT) - - Psalms 37:7." Bible Gateway, Tyndale House Publishers, 2015, www.biblegateway.com. Accessed 13 Nov. 2023.

"New Living Translation (NLT) - - Philippians 4:19." Bible Gateway, Tyndale House Publishers, 2015, www.biblegateway.com. Accessed **9 Sept. 2024**.

"New Living Translation (NLT) - - Proverbs 3:6." Bible Gateway,

Tyndale House Publishers, 2015, www.biblegateway.com. Accessed **10 Sept. 2024**.

Palmer, Pamela. "How Pray without Ceasing - Bible Verse Meaning Explained." *Bible Study Tools*, Salem Web Network, 6 Mar. 2020, www.biblestudytools.com/bible-study/topical-studies/can-we-really-pray-without-ceasing.html. Accessed 13 Nov. 2023.

Piper, John. *The Justification of God*. Baker Publishing Group, 1993, Kindle Edition, pp. 100, 112, 133-134.

"Pride Definition & Meaning." *Merriam-Webster*, Merriam-Webster, www.merriam-webster.com/dictionary/pride. Accessed 14 Nov. 2023.

Saba, Brent. *The Almighty: God's Holy Attributes & Their Meaning for Your Life*. Kindle Direct Publishing, 2019, Kindle Edition, p. 24.

Seltzer, Leon F. "Righteous vs. Self-Righteous | Psychology Today." *Psychology Today*, 13 Jan. 2021, www.psychologytoday.com/us/blog/evolution-the-self/202101/righteous-vs-self-righteous. Accessed 13 Nov. 2023.

Smith, Joseph Fielding. *Answers to Gospel Questions: Volumes 1-5 (Volume 1 - - Multiply and Replenish)*. Deseret Book

Company, 2012, Kindle Edition.

Spurgeon, C H. "Admin." *Precept Austin*, 2023, www.preceptaustin.org/matthew_619-21. Accessed 13 Nov. 2023.

Stewart, Don. "What Was God Doing before He Created the Universe?" Blue Letter Bible. 24 Apr. 2007. Web. 14 Nov. 2023. <https://www.blueletterbible.org/faq/don_stewart/don_stewart_643.cfm>.

Tarrants, Thomas A. "Pride and Humility." *C.S. Lewis Institute*, 18 May 2022, www.cslewisinstitute.org/resources/pride-and-humility/. Accessed 13 Nov. 2023.

"The Message (MSG) - - 2 Peter 1:5-9." Bible Gateway, Eugene H. Peterson, 2018, www.biblegateway.com. Accessed 13 Nov. 2023.

"The Message (MSG) - - Deuteronomy 8:17, 18." Bible Gateway, Eugene H. Peterson, 2018, www.biblegateway.com. Accessed 13 Nov. 2023.

"The Message (MSG) - - Ephesians 3:20-21." Bible Gateway, Eugene H. Peterson, 2018, www.biblegateway.com. Accessed 13 Nov. 2023.

"The Message (MSG) - - Hebrews 11:6." Bible Gateway, Eugene H.

Peterson, 2018, www.biblegateway.com. Accessed 13 Nov. 2023.

"The Message (MSG) - - Proverbs 14:13." Bible Gateway, Eugene H. Peterson, 2018, www.biblegateway.com. Accessed 13 Nov. 2023.

"The Message (MSG) - - Romans 7:24." Bible Gateway, Eugene H. Peterson, 2018, www.biblegateway.com. Accessed **10 Sept. 2024**.

"The Message (MSG) - - Romans 12:3." Bible Gateway, Eugene H. Peterson, 2018, www.biblegateway.com. Accessed 13 Nov. 2023.

"The Voice (VOICE) - - 2 Peter 1:4." Bible Gateway, Thomas Nelson, 2012, www.biblegateway.com. Accessed **10 Sept. 2024**.

"The Voice (VOICE) - - Colossians 1:16." Bible Gateway, Thomas Nelson, 2012, www.biblegateway.com. Accessed **10 Sept. 2024**.

"The Voice (VOICE) - - Ephesians 4:26-27." Bible Gateway, Thomas Nelson, 2012, www.biblegateway.com. Accessed **10 Sept. 2024**.

"The Voice (VOICE) - - Hebrews 11:1." Bible Gateway, Thomas Nelson, 2012, www.biblegateway.com. Accessed **9 Sept.**

2024.

"The Voice (VOICE) - - Isaiah 40:22." Bible Gateway, Thomas Nelson, 2012, www.biblegateway.com. Accessed **10 Sept. 2024.**

"The Voice (VOICE) - - James 1:14-15." Bible Gateway, Thomas Nelson, 2012, www.biblegateway.com. Accessed **10 Sept. 2024.**

"The Voice (VOICE) - - Job 26:7." Bible Gateway, Thomas Nelson, 2012, www.biblegateway.com. Accessed **9 Sept. 2024.**

"The Voice (VOICE) - - Matthew 5:16." Bible Gateway, Thomas Nelson, 2012, www.biblegateway.com. Accessed **0 Sept. 2024.**

"The Voice (VOICE) - - Philippians 4:19." Bible Gateway, Thomas Nelson, 2012, www.biblegateway.com. Accessed **9 Sept. 2024.**

"The Voice (VOICE) - - Psalm 19:1; 32:8; 33:9." Bible Gateway, Thomas Nelson, 2012, www.biblegateway.com. Accessed **10 Sept. 2024.**

Tozer, A. W. *Knowledge of the Holy: The Attributes of God (AW Tozer Series Book 2).* SHJBOOX, 2023, Kindle Edition, pp. 73, 74, 87, 88.

"Tree of Life Version (TLV) - - Daniel 11:32." Bible Gateway, The

Messianic Jewish Family Bible Society, 2015, www.biblegateway.com. Accessed 13 Nov. 2023.

"Tree of Life Version (TLV) - - Genesis 11:4." Bible Gateway, The Messianic Jewish Family Bible Society, 2015, www.biblegateway.com. Accessed 13 Nov. 2023.

US Department of Commerce, NOAA. "Why Do We Have Seasons?" *National Weather Service*, NOAA's National Weather Service, 5 Mar. 2023, www.weather.gov/lmk/seasons. Accessed 13 Nov. 2023.

Zuckerman, Phil. "What Is Secular Humanism?" *Psychology Today*, Sussex Publishers, 12 Feb. 2020, www.psychologytoday.com/us/blog/the-secular-life/202002/what-is-secular-humanism. Accessed 13 Nov. 2023.

About The Author

Dr. Gwen E. Brannum is an advocate of education, and she is committed to being a life-long student. After graduating from High School in Detroit Michigan, she has continued her educational journey by attending community colleges, universities, technical institutions, Bible Colleges, and Seminary. As a result, Dr. Brannum has gained a wealth of insight both spiritually and naturally. From a spiritual perspective, she has received an Associate of Theology, Bachelor of Science in Biblical Studies, Master of Arts in Christian Education, Doctor of Ministry in Christian Counseling, and a Doctor of Philosophy in Christian Business.

Dr. Brannum is also an entrepreneur and humanitarian. As an entrepreneur, she has founded various organizations including Apostolic Pentecostal Truth Ministry, Inc. (1992), Apostolic Pentecostal Truth Ministries, Inc. (2005), Gwen Brannum Ministries, LLC. (2005), Proven to Succeed Ministries, Inc. (2011), Proven to Succeed Day Care, Inc. (2011), and Proven to Succeed Child Development Center, Inc. (2015) - in honor of the boundless Master Builder. As a Christian business owner, Dr. Brannum declares the key to her success is adhering to - *The Master Builder's Blueprint for Building Enduring Wealth.*

www.ingramcontent.com/pod-product-compliance
Lightning Source LLC
Chambersburg PA
CBHW071322120626

46546CB00002B/403